Donated by

Alice Fish

2014

St. James Library
131 N. State Street
Painesville, Ohio 44077

The Abbey of Gethsemani:
Place of Peace and Paradox

Also by Dianne Aprile:
The Things We Don't Forget

THE ABBEY OF

Gethsemani

PLACE *of* PEACE

and PARADOX

*150 Years in the Life of America's
Oldest Trappist Monastery*

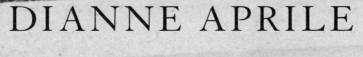

DIANNE APRILE

TROUT LILY PRESS

1903

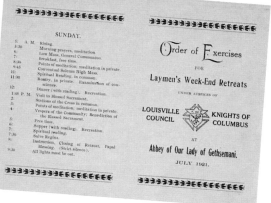

First published in the United States in 1998
by Trout Lily Press

Library of Congress Catalogue Number: 97-61455
ISBN: 0-9642802-1-3

Book design by Julie Breeding,
Plaschke Design Group, Louisville, Kentucky

PICTURED ON TABLE OF CONTENTS PAGE: *The marble
altar piece installed in the early 1920s, and a crosier,
consisting of 7,000 pieces of inlaid wood, made for
Dom Eutropius by a Gethsemani monk.*

TROUT LILY
PRESS

Entrance to the Abbey of Our Lady of Gethsemani, which celebrated its diamond jubilee.

Brother Alexis of Alsace-Lorraine welcoming Father Felton of Louisville to the Abbey.

The well on the Abbey grounds.

His Eminence Dennis Cardinal Dougherty (left) and Father Edmond M. Obrecht, for twenty-five years Abbot of Gethsemani and for fifty years a priest.

Triple Celebration at Gethsemani Abbey, Home of the Silent Trappists

—Photos by C. Betz, Staff Photographer

The postmaster, his barred window and his showcase filled with curios which he sells to visitors.

Over the hills and far away are Louisville and worldly ways.

(Left) A quaint corner in the Abbey, where the monks keep their hats and shoes.

Trappist monks leading the procession to the Pontifical Mass.

"Now I saw the monastery from within, from the church floor, so to speak, not from the visitors' gallery . . . not from the shiny and well-heated Guest House. Now I was face to face with monks that belonged not to some dream, not to some medieval novel, but to cold and inescapable reality. . . . All the details, good and bad, pleasant and unpleasant, were there for me to observe at close range."

– Thomas Merton, "The Seven Storey Mountain"

To our mothers, Sissy, Ruth and Nancy
– D.A., Br. J.B. and J.B.

PREFACE: A CALL to CHANGE

IN THE AUTUMN OF 1990, I MADE A TRIP THAT
changed my life. With a tape recorder, notebook and
my overnight bag on the seat beside me, I drove my
mini-van down the meandering 55-mile stretch of inter-
state highway and country road that
connects my home in Louisville to the
Abbey of Gethsemani. I was on a magazine assignment, making the first of two
visits I had arranged over the telephone.

> "THERE IS IN ALL THINGS . . .
> A HIDDEN WHOLENESS"
> THOMAS MERTON

I arrived that October day blessedly free of precon-
ceptions. Unlike many who come to the abbey for the
first time, I knew almost nothing about its rich Kentucky history or its European roots or its centuries-old
Cistercian traditions. I had only recently become
acquainted with the place, having encountered it,
peripherally, in the journals of Thomas Merton. It was,
oddly enough, those spellbinding diaries (and not the
bestseller *The Seven Storey Mountain* nor, for that matter,
my 12 years of Catholic education) that had introduced
me to what little I knew of Gethsemani.

There is a peculiar kind of pleasure in looking back
and tracking the roundabout paths that lead us to the
work we are supposed to be doing. In this case, it was
the power of words written by a monk who was dead by
the time I read them that triggered the curiosity, that

inspired the assignment, that provoked the return visits,
that fueled the spiritual journey, that cemented the
friendships, that led to the hours and days and months
and years of inquiry and exploration and delight and
discovery that became the book you now
hold in your hands.

Eight years after that first visit, I
concede that I am still learning about my
subject, the 150-year-old proto-abbey of
North America. Who would believe so many stories
could come out of one house? Particularly one with a
wall built solidly around it, a sign to outsiders of its separation from the world. Walls and cloister notwith-
standing, I have come to believe nine out of 10 Kentuckians have a personal story about the abbey, and much of
the rest of the world has at the very least a second-hand
tale to tell. Visitors clearly don't forget a visit to Trappist,
Kentucky; nor do they keep the details to themselves.
The obvious challenge in writing a history of Gethsemani, then, is to know which stories to leave out and
which to include. Beyond that, there is the task of illu-
minating a way of life that frankly defies definition.

Early in my research, I was fortunate to find among
the abundant treasures in the abbey archives an old
pamphlet concerning the history of the community.

Instinctively, without really knowing how profoundly accurate and comforting it would prove to be, I jotted down this sentence and slipped it into a file. Father Louis, as Merton was known to his monastic brothers, wrote it:

There are things about Gethsemani that cannot be put into words whatsoever; still less can they be comprehensively published for the edification of multitudes.

Yet, Father Louis never stopped trying to find the words that might capture the essence of Gethsemani; nor have I. With the help of the community's talented and devoted archivist, Brother Joshua Brands, I have set out on these pages to narrate the story of the oldest Trappist abbey in the United States. This is not an academic history, footnoted and annotated for the scholars among us; nor is it a "romanced history," as Father Raymond Flanagan, Gethsemani's great popularizer of Trappist lore, liked to call his historical novels.

Think of this book as personal history, as family memoir, as the collective biography of a community over time. More than once, listening to the recollections of Gethsemani's monks or reading their letters, I have thought of my own childhood, sitting at my grandmother's round table, receiving the wisdom of aunts and uncles and friends of the family, allowing their reminiscences to form a narrative in my young and willing heart.

This is how we humans experience history, whether it is that of our nation, our world or our universe. It is not by memorizing a timeline or a chronological listing of dates and events that we learn our story. We embrace it as a narrative with a beginning, a middle, various crescendos and crises and denouements, with characters

of weakness and of strength, with geographical, economic and political subplots, recurring themes, conflicts, resolutions and, above all, meaning and significance. It is through this process that facts and figures and circumstance weave together and create the richly colored, deliberately textured tapestry we call history.

For three years, I have come and gone through the gates that separate the monks of Gethsemani from the visiting public. On my way to the archives, a densely packed two-room suite on the third floor of the library, I have passed monks baking, biking, building, mowing, walking, jogging, weeding, sweeping, cleaning, praying. A gracious and generous community has permitted me to freely enter cloistered territory that once spelled excommunication for the female trespasser. So seldom did a woman step across that boundary line in the past that when she did, it made the front pages of Kentucky's newspapers.

In 1901, when Kentucky Gov. J.C.W. Beckham's wife became the first woman to enter Gethsemani's cloister, reporters hauled out their purplest prose to communicate the extraordinary nature of such a social call. Editors illustrated their stories with handsome portraits of the First Lady in all her feminine finery.

I remember well the day I came across those yellowed, fraying newspaper accounts of Mrs. Beckham's once-in-a-lifetime visit. I was wearing work clothes — a sweater and jeans; and my hands were covered in fine dust from rooting through storage boxes. My appearances on the "private" side of the cloister had long since ceased to surprise anyone; my acceptance by the community had been helped along by the fact that a Trappistine nun had moved into the monastery not long after my

book research began. I recall smiling at Mrs. Beckham and thanking her for the graphic reminder of just how much has changed at Gethsemani over the course of 150 years.

Indeed, when it comes to change, Gethsemani's history is one of paradox: within a context of commitment and tradition, the abbey exists in constant flux. At their time of solemn profession, Trappists take a vow of stability, a promise to remain a part of their particular community for the rest of their lives. Cistercian life is about constancy, fidelity, steadiness, endurance. Their way of life dates back to 1098. Their daily routines, the prayers they pray, the psalms they chant, are the same, in large part, as those that made up their brothers' lives 900 years ago.

Yet, Gethsemani is where I learned to accept change not merely as an inescapable fact of life but as the gift that it is: a reason for hope, an invitation to trust, a great

grace. It's a mystery, and mysteries are best handled by way of stories. Here is mine:

At the end of my second trip to Gethsemani, when my magazine reporting was complete and all that remained to be done was the writing, I asked a monk who had been showing me around the monastery if he would take me to the one place I had not had a chance to visit. I wanted to go to the woods across Monks Road and see the statues I had been told about, the bronze sculptures by Walker Hancock representing Christ on his knees in the Garden of Gethsemani and his apostles asleep nearby. My guide was happy to show them to me. I arranged it so the statues would be my last activity before heading back to my office.

The scene was more beautiful than I expected: the deeply moving sculptures, the feeling of being wrapped in the arms of the thick woods surrounding us, the eerie

creaking of the high branches of the towering cedars that encircled the statue of Christ. I remember my guide telling me to look up at the green tops of the cedars wind-tossed against a background of blue autumn sky. "When I look at them this way," he said, "they remind me of the ocean at home in Massachusetts." We sat a while, in silence, and then we parted ways.

A few years later, after I had stopped counting the times I had driven the 55 miles from Louisville to Gethsemani and back, a freak summer windstorm blew through Nelson County. Some claimed it was a tornado, and judging by what it accomplished at Gethsemani, it would not surprise me if they were right. It ripped the roof off one wing of the monastery. It shredded the evergreens in the retreat house garden. It toppled a silo. And across Monks Road, it took down the thick forest leading to and surrounding the statues.

I heard about the storm and put off driving out to see the damage for as long as I could. When I finally witnessed it, I literally winced at the sight of so many broken trees. When I looked out the retreat house dining room windows, I ached for those giant firs I used to watch take shape, one by one, as the sun rose and the early morning darkness lifted.

But the greatest shock was seeing the statues. They were no longer hidden in a grove of cedars nor surrounded by woods. Now they stood out in the distance, stark and desolate, as I approached them on foot. At first I thought I was lost, so different was the lay of the land. The only hint of the trees that had once dominated the area was the tangle of split limbs and ravaged trunks that I had to climb over to reach the statues. I felt disoriented and grief-stricken. My refuge, the place I treasured for its solitude and peace, would never be the same. Yet I found, to a man, the monks I expressed these feelings to were philosophical about the devastation. Nature has its own way of pruning, one told me. It's really more beautiful now, another said. This will allow for new growth, said someone else. Change is healthy. Change is necessary. Change is good.

Think of the French monks of Melleray Abbey who took their vows of stability, promising to stay put in their lovely Loire Valley monastery, with the 12th century church and the lake with geese swimming in it, not far from where many of them grew up in Europe's precarious post-revolutionary years. Imagine the life they had every reason to expect, simple and straightforward and situated in a region whose landscape and history they knew by heart. And then envision the day they left all that and set out on foot on the first leg of a journey that would take them across an ocean, up a mighty river, into a wilderness known as Kentucky, where their silence would be magnified by the vastness of the countryside and their solitude sealed by their lack of familiarity with English. This is the legacy of the immigrant monks who founded the Abbey of Gethsemani in December 1848: the ability to embrace change and not fear it, to look for God's will and God's love in every unexpected turn in the road.

Those first few years of getting to know Gethsemani, I had mistakenly – and for the most part unconsciously – embraced it as a place where time stood still. This is a common illusion, a romantic and false first impression of the monastic life as a refuge. What unnerved me about the ravaged landscape, I now understand, was that it profoundly contradicted my fantasy of Gethsemani as a community protected from life's upheavals and vicissitudes. The storm made me see that, in fact, Trappist life – like the faith in God that inspires it and grounds it – is ever-evolving, growing, developing, expanding, deepening, changing.

Branches break, paths diverge, dark history repeats itself, but always there is that "hidden wholeness:" that mystery of redemption that Merton linked to every vestige of creation; that "meek namelessness," as he called it, whose will it is to restore the shattered peace with forgiveness and love.

Do not expect to discover some holy vision of tranquil retreat connecting the stories of this 150-year-old Trappist community. Rather, it is the enduring impulse to reclaim a wounded world that binds its history and informs its future.

This is the call of Gethsemani, the unspoken invitation that year upon year draws monk and visitor alike to its cloistered corridors and wooded hills – the chance to change.

DESERT FATHERS, EARLY MONKS
and CISTERCIAN REFORMERS
275-1796

STRICTLY SPEAKING, THE HISTORY OF THE ABBEY OF Gethsemani commences on Oct. 26, 1848, just before dawn, when a band of French monks from the Abbey of Melleray set out from their homeland to found a monastery in Kentucky. An extraordinary year was coming to a close as they said their good-byes on the dirt road outside their beloved cloister.

Indeed, it was an exceptional era in which they lived. The year before the founding of Gethsemani, Frederick Douglass published the first edition of his abolitionist newspaper; Karl Marx proclaimed his *Communist Manifesto*; and farmers had their first look at a steam-powered cotton gin. A few months before the Melleray monks arrived in Nelson County, the town of Seneca Falls, New York, hosted a Women's Rights Convention, the first gathering of its kind in the nation. Just days before the Trappists set foot on American soil, Prince Louis Napoleon Bonaparte was elected president of France, and the Pope was exiled from Rome. Change – dramatic and far-reaching – was in the air.

But to begin Gethsemani's history in 1848 would be like telling your life story without mentioning your parents or grandparents, your first home or your family's lineage. Without this background, there would be no context for what came later.

And that is why we begin not in 1848, when the Trappists from Melleray arrived at the Falls of the Ohio River; nor in 1803, when an earlier party of French Trappists tried but failed to found a monastery in the wilds of Kentucky. We cannot even launch our story in the 17th century when Trappists first came into being as a reform of the Cistercian Order; nor in 1098, when the Cistercian Order itself was founded at Citeaux in eastern France.

To really understand the story, we must look back a full 17 centuries to the first Christian monks, the desert hermits who lived in poverty on the margins of society, seeking God alone. In their faith and way of life, we find the prototype for the Trappist monks of Gethsemani.

In the Beginning

In Egypt in the year 285, a young man gave away all he owned and moved to the desert. His name was Anthony, and he was, by all accounts, a child of comfortable peasant stock. A theologian and author of the era, Athanasius of Alexandria, popularized Anthony's dramatic story and created in him the world's first heroic monk. He was later canonized a saint and is now sometimes referred to as Anthony the Great, but he certainly would have preferred the title of Anthony the Humble. He was a man who advocated a radical simplicity, in keeping with the life and teachings of Christ. He lived as a hermit: fasting, praying and sharing whatever he had with anyone who needed it. The love of God is all he sought to possess.

As extreme as his decision may seem to us today, it made perfect sense to many of his contemporaries. Men and women alike followed his lead. Knowing how challenging the solitary life could be, Anthony came up with a simple routine of prayer and work to give order to his disciples' days. It was the first monastic "rule." Anthony eventually moved deeper into the desert but continued to attract followers and remained a force in the early church for four decades. He is known as the father of monasticism.

Pachomius, another well-known hermit of the era, attracted followers too, but he organized his disciples into communities. These groups of men and women shared a common, or *cenobitic* life under a rule of obedience. Once the two branches of monasticism were established, deserts in Egypt, Persia, Arabia and Palestine blossomed with monks living separately in solitude or together in communities.

In *The Wisdom of the Desert*, Thomas Merton's collection of sayings from 4th-century hermits, he describes the first monks as unpretentious believers who "had come into the desert to be themselves, their ordinary selves." This is one of the great paradoxes of monasticism. What the world considers an extraordinary gesture – an individual's deliberate withdrawal from the world and surrender of will – is, to the monk, the most basic and essential of activities. It is a decision to embrace the commonplace and customary with love; to seek God in the humdrum details and random relationships of everyday life.

Anthony's quest for greater simplicity was born out of his desire to imitate Christ, but it paralleled other spiritual trends of the day. By the time Anthony entered the desert, certain Syrian Christians had begun forming groups in which they exercised strict religious discipline, including celibacy – but without separating themselves from society. It's likely these early monks were also influenced by the practices of two Jewish groups, the Essenes and Therepeutae, as well as by Buddhism and other strains of asceticism, including the Neoplatonic.

There were political reasons, too, for monasticism's

Tome 1.

Saint Antoine.

ABOVE: *St. Anthony at prayer.* LEFT: *12th-century Italian antiphonary, or choir book, originally used at the Abbey of Morimond and acquired by Gethsemani's Dom Edmond Obrecht as part of his collection of rare Cistercian manuscripts.*

appeal. In 312, the Roman Emperor Constantine granted official status to the Church for the first time. This concerned some members of the once-persecuted community. They feared an increasingly privileged status might erode their religious fervor and distract them from the rigorous moral demands of the Gospel. The desert monasteries, by contrast, offered support for a more disciplined and thoughtful lifestyle.

The popular appeal of monasticism was critical to the growth and development of the early Church. Pachomius is said to have attracted as many as 9,000

men and women to desert monasteries. Some houses, like that at Tabenna, were enormous in size. Bishops were chosen from among their ranks. A body of monastic literature grew up. *Sayings of the Fathers*, a collection of stories passed down from Anthony and his contemporaries, circulated widely in the 5th century, as did the work of Augustine of Hippo and John Cassian, two important chroniclers of desert spirituality.

Monasticism officially arrived in the West in 362 when Martin of Tours founded the first French monastery near Poitiers. But it was Benedict of Nursia,

two centuries later, who created the unique framework that distinguishes Western monasticism from other forms. Blessed with profound insight into human behavior, Benedict wrote The Rule for his monks at Monte Cassino, the Italian monastery he established in 529, which later became the chief house of the Benedictine Order. He was influenced by both the writings of Cassian – particularly his descriptions of the early Egyptian monks – and an anonymous work that circulated about the same time, the *Regula Magistri* or *Rule of the Master.*

What was it that made The Rule of St. Benedict

such a success? Why, by the millennium, was it the norm in monastic houses across Europe? Why is it still the basis of most Western communities, including the Abbey of Gethsemani?

In The Rule, Benedict successfully balanced the spiritual requirements of the contemplative journey with the practical necessities of running a monastery. Life was organized around the disciplines of prayer, manual labor and Scripture reading. Benedict's monks agreed to live as the poorest of the poor, to remain unmarried and abstinent from sexual activity, to do what their superiors told them and to stay put in one

port. In 594, Pope Gregory the Great publicly applauded The Rule as he dispatched monks to England to establish that nation's first Benedictine monastery at Canterbury. Two hundred years later, Charlemagne imposed The Rule on all monastic communities within his empire. By the dawn of the millennium, Benedict's blueprint dominated Western abbeys, except in Ireland, where The Rule's emphasis on solitude and seclusion clashed with Celtic monasticism's evangelistic streak.

YET, EVEN WITH THE WIDESPREAD ADOPTION OF THE Rule, there was great diversity among Medieval Benedictine orders. Experiments and reforms led to frequent modifications of monastic life. The Abbey of Cluny, founded in France in 910, was a breeding ground for such change; its family of monasteries became a major force in society. At their peak, the Cluniacs, or Black Monks, as they were known, controlled 1,000 monasteries and were known for their splendid ritual and liturgy. Over time, however, they strayed significantly from the path of simplicity outlined by Benedict.

In reaction to the imbalances of Cluny, the Carthusian and Camaldolese reforms of the 11th century sought to restore the lost contemplative aspects of The Rule.

But by far the most far-reaching monastic reform of the 11th century was the Cistercian movement, which was born in a marshland outside Dijon, France, at a place called Citeaux. It is to this 900-year-old clan of contemplatives that the Abbey of Gethsemani traces its monastic ideal.

OPPOSITE: Map of French Benedictine monasteries. ABOVE: Portrait of St. Benedict. RIGHT: The Rule of St. Benedict, followed today by the monks of Gethsemani.

monastic house for the rest of their lives. The Rule stressed simplicity and moderation, virtues Benedict had come to appreciate during his years as a hermit, prior to founding Monte Cassino.

Benedict reduced the amount of time monks prayed together in church, for example, and increased the hours they spent at work in the fields. Extreme fasting was discouraged; silence and contemplation were nurtured. Benedict cared more about a monk's interior spiritual development than outward demonstrations of self-denial.

The Rule also won some important political sup-

Above: *An aerial photograph of the Abbey of Citeaux, taken in the early part of this century.* Left: *The Order's great preacher and saint, Bernard of Clairvaux, illuminated on the page of an early manuscript.* Opposite: *A 12th-century tile fragment from the Abbey of Citeaux.*

THE STORY of the CISTERCIANS

THREE YEARS INTO THE MEDIEVAL BLOODBATH KNOWN as The First Crusade, a band of 21 French monks and their abbot, Robert, set out on a holy war of their own. Leaving their monastery at Molesme in Burgundy, they headed north. Their quest was as old as Anthony's, as elemental as Adam's: to retrieve what had been lost. Specifically they sought a return to the purity of The Rule of St. Benedict.

They set up shop at Citeaux, which was, at the time, a marshy woodland not far from Dijon in eastern France. The Latin word for Citeaux is *Cistercium*, and so the men who settled there came to be known as Cistercians.

The monks who arrived at Citeaux on Palm Sunday 1098, were determined to live modestly. They were frustrated by the Cluniacs' "refinements" of The Rule: the downplay of manual labor; the meals that sidestepped Benedict's dietary restrictions; the fur-lined jackets and ornamental garments that contradicted The Rule's emphasis on poverty and humility.

The monks of Citeaux, like Benedict before them, simplified their prayer life. They pared back their diet; slept on beds of straw; built their church of stone without adornment; wore robes of undyed wool. That last habit earned them their nickname, The White Monks.

They were striving for the harmony that Benedict

> "... THE FERVOR AND SUCCESS OF A RELIGIOUS ORDER DEPENDS ENTIRELY ON HOW CLOSE IT CAN MANAGE TO KEEP TO THE OBJECT FOR WHICH IT WAS FOUNDED."
>
> THOMAS MERTON, THE WATERS OF SILOE

had so wisely built into his Rule. Labor would co-exist with prayer; the interior rewards of contemplative life would find their balance in the physical rigors of community membership. One of Citeaux's complaints against Cluny was that the monastery benefited from an economic system that exploited the poor. Like the desert fathers before them, the Cistercians detached themselves from popular culture. They did not operate schools or run parishes or take in children to groom as future monks, as some monastic communities did. And virtually from the start, Cistercians divided their communities into two groups – choir monks, who were generally priests, and *conversi*, or lay brothers. The lay brothers, who lived separately, spent more time at manual labor and were exempt from choral services.

In a departure from contemporary monastic practice, Citeaux also perfected a "filiation" system that bonded motherhouses to daughterhouses and allowed for orderly expansion. By requiring annual visits to foundations and by convening all abbots for annual legislative meetings known as General Chapters, the Cistercians maintained uniformity throughout the order, from architectural principles and musical styles to interpretations of The Rule. They were familiar with the corruption that arises when an individual abbot

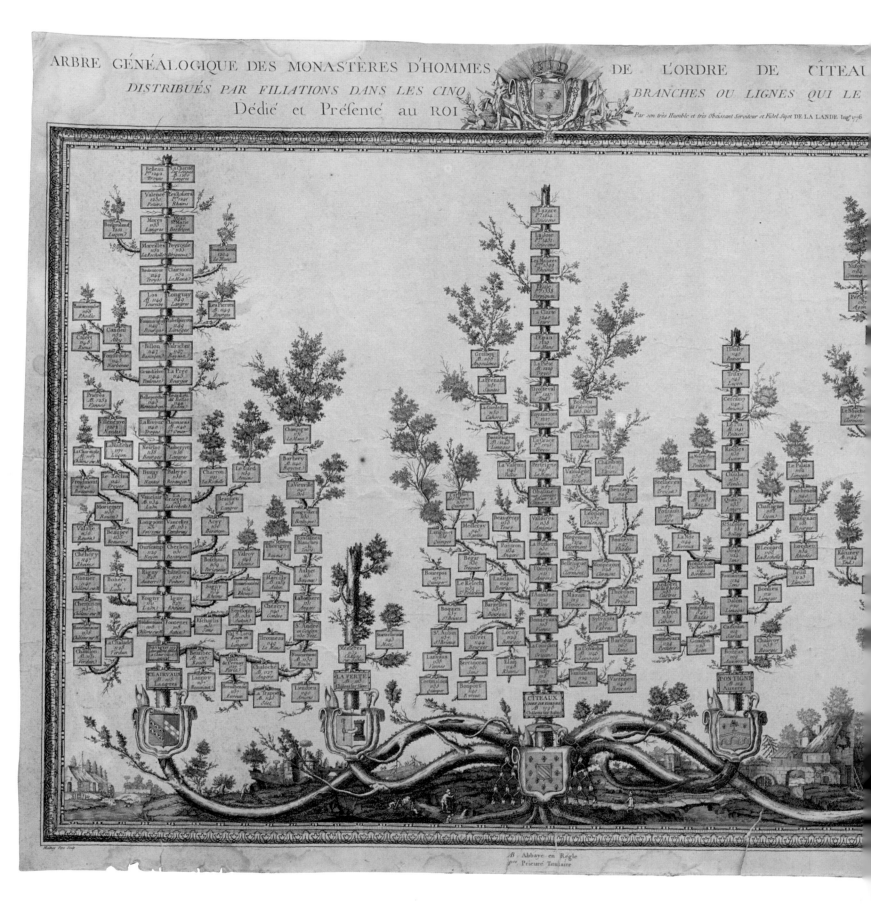

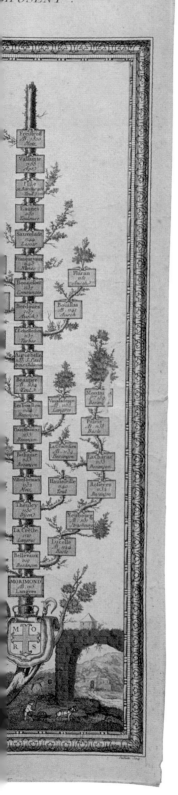

LEFT: *A family tree from 1776, depicting the growth of the Cistercian Order.* ABOVE: *Cistercian founder Robert of Molesme, shown in a Gethsemani stained-glass window.*

becomes too powerful or when houses stray from purpose. The Cistercian constitution was designed to impede such abuses.

CITEAUX FLOURISHED FROM THE START. ALTHOUGH Dom Robert's tenure as abbot lasted only one year (he was recalled by his community at Molesme and returned obediently), he had brought two strong leaders with him: Dom Alberic, who followed Dom Robert, and Stephen Harding, a British monk who succeeded Alberic at his death a decade later.

By 1113, Citeaux had grown large and strong enough to give birth to its first foundation, the Abbey of La Ferte. About that same time, a young nobleman by the name of Bernard entered Citeaux with a group of friends and relatives he had persuaded to accompany him. Within a few years, Bernard was abbot of Citeaux's third foundation, the Abbey of Clairvaux. A mystic as well as a tremendously effective spiritual writer and preacher, Bernard of Clairvaux wrote several masterpieces of monastic literature, including his unfinished series of sermons on the *Song of Songs*.

Though he was a great advocate of the contemplative aspects of monasticism and wrote poignantly of their rewards, Bernard had little time of his own to spend in quiet reflection. He wrote treatise after treatise on church issues of the day and traveled widely, usually at the behest of popes. He preached The Second Crusade across northern Europe and directed the founding of 68 new houses during his 38 years as abbot. He died at Clairvaux in 1153.

OVER THE NEXT SEVERAL CENTURIES, THE CISTERCIAN movement matured into one of the most powerful monastic orders of the Middle Ages. Through its contributions to choral music, religious literature and church architecture, the order exerted a dynamic spiritual and cultural influence on Western life.

By the time of Bernard's death, Citeaux had generated more than 300 Cistercian houses for women and men throughout France, Italy, Germany, England, Wales and Ireland. Its first monastery for women, the Abbey of Tart, was founded near Citeaux in 1125. Just as the early bishops often came from the ranks of the desert fathers, now popes were chosen from among Cistercian abbeys for men, which numbered 750 by the year 1300. By the 15th century, the order began grouping its monasteries into regional congregations by geographical location.

But the larger, wealthier and more politically connected that Citeaux grew, the more its contemplative spirit suffered. Cistercians set up offices in towns like Dijon to market their products, which included wine, grain and wool. The effort it took to keep up with these material pursuits left little time for the quiet reflection and silent prayer that Bernard had so rightly characterized as the heart of Cistercian spirituality in his sermons and treatises. Accepting tithes or earning income from parishes – activities forbidden by the founders of the Order – became common practice.

Meanwhile, political tides were shifting, too. The Protestant Reformation of the 16th century led to the suppression of monasteries, seizure of their land and years of bloody conflict throughout Europe and England. Marauders plundered the Abbey of Citeaux in 1589 and again in 1595.

By the 17th century, a political practice known as *commendam* allowed for the control of monasteries by noble families. It was not uncommon for secular princes

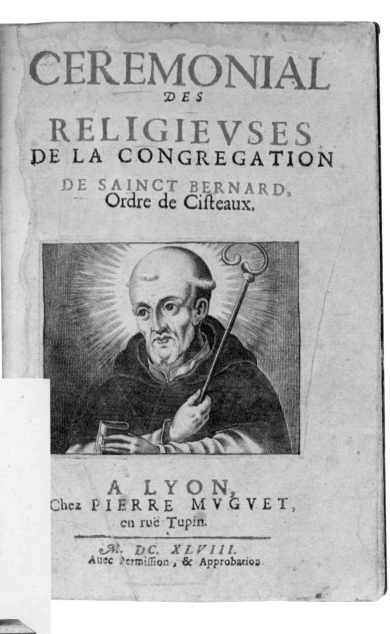

ABOVE: *A Cistercian book of ceremonies, printed in 1648.* LEFT: *The abbess of the Abbey of Tart, the Order's first Cistercian monastery for women.*

30

MONASTICISM GROWS

285: Anthony retires to Egyptian desert and attracts disciples.

312: Roman Emperor Constantine gives Christianity official status.

320: Pachomius organizes desert monks into communities.

362: The first Western monastery is founded by Martin of Tours at Poitiers.

433: Attila becomes leader of the Huns.

513: Mt. Vesuvius erupts a second time, again burying Pompeii.

529: St. Benedict writes The Rule for monks at Monte Cassino.

610: Mohammed teaches new religion, to be called Islam, at Mecca.

633: Christian churches in Asia are turned into Muslim mosques.

709: Mont St. Michel begins construction.

793: Vikings raid Irish monasteries.

800: Yiddish is invented.

868: World's first printed book is published.

910: Cluny founded, becomes center of monastic reform.

1098: Citeaux is founded as reform of Cluny.

1099: First Crusade ends: 40,000 die as Jerusalem falls.

1113: Bernard of Clairvaux enters Citeaux.

1125: Citeaux founds first abbey for nuns at Tart.

1136: Gothic architecture appears in Europe.

1145: Melleray is founded.

1521: Martin Luther is excommunicated as heretic.

1534: Henry VIII breaks with church, suppresses monasteries.

1542: Inquisition is led by Jesuits and Dominicans.

1589: Citeaux is plundered (again in 1595).

A page from the Gutenburg Chronicle, part of Gethsemani's collection of rare manuscripts, portraying the founding of the Cistercian Order.

1623: Strict Observance is formed in France.

1664: Armand Jean de Rance, abbot of La Trappe, takes vows of Strict Observance.

1789: French Revolution shuts down monastic life in France.

1791: Dom Augustin de Lestrange leaves La Trappe for La Valsainte, Switzerland.

1792: Melleray is closed down by French Revolution.

1796: Augustin de Lestrange forms first Trappistines.

FONDATION *de l'Abbaye de la Trappe, par* ROTROU, *Comte du Perche l'an 1140. sous le Pontif*
Roy de France ; 42. ans apres la fondation de Cisteaux ; 25. ans apres celle de Clervaux .

to bequeath abbeys to their friends as payment for favors. This abuse resulted in "commendatory" abbeys which bore little resemblance to the real thing, and absentee abbots who were really not abbots at all.

Against this backdrop of decline, another cycle of reforms grew up, leading to a split within the Cistercian order. On one hand, The Cistercians of the Strict Observance opposed the relaxed Rule that had come to be Citeaux's norm, while followers of The Common Observance supported it.

Innocent II. et sous le Regne de Louis VII.

ABOVE: *An 18th-century engraving of the founding of La Trappe in 1120.* TOP RIGHT: *Scene from the abbey's chapter, illustrating the revival of the Chapter of Faults under de Rance.* BOTTOM RIGHT: *The refectory.*

The most remarkable of the Strict Observance firebrands was Armand Jean de Rance, a commendatory abbot who at the age of 12 had control of several monasteries, including La Grande Trappe. Educated at The Sorbonne, De Rance eventually became a Cistercian monk of The Strict Observance and served as abbot of La Trappe until his death in 1700.

A dramatic and uncompromising leader, De Rance initiated an exacting regimen of discipline and penance at La Trappe. His interpretation of the Strict Observance reform gave it the vitality it would need to survive the coming years of political turmoil. Those who followed it were dubbed "Trappists."

LE R. P. DOM AUGUSTIN DE LESTRANGE

DESPITE THE RENEWED VIGOR THAT DE RANCE'S reform brought to Cistercian life, monasticism was hardly out of the woods. In 1789, the French Revolution erupted. Once again monasteries were abolished and property confiscated. Worship of God was outlawed. When Trappist monks refused to sign oaths of allegiance to the openly atheistic government, they were imprisoned in chain gangs or exiled to penal colonies. Many were executed or died from diseases contracted in captivity.

At La Trappe at the time of the Revolution, the novice master was a man named Augustin de Lestrange. Determined to keep the Trappist reform alive, he fled France with 25 of his monks. The group ultimately found refuge in an abandoned Carthusian monastery at La Valsainte, Switzerland. Here Dom Augustin and his small community lived in even harsher circumstances and under a more exacting interpretation of the Strict Observance than they had at La Trappe. Their work was more arduous, and the climate less hospitable. They ate meagerly and slept little. Despite the hardships they faced, the Trappists were able to

ABOVE: *Augustin de Lestrange.*
RIGHT: *Armand Jean de Rance.*
OPPOSITE: *The Abbey of Melleray, the motherhouse of the Abbey of Gethsemani.*

Vue de l'Abbaye de La Trappe de Melleray près Nantes.
(prise du Nord-Ouest.)

make several foundations, including one in Lulworth, England. In 1796, they formed the first Trappistine community.

Coincidentally, about the time that the monks of La Trappe were fleeing France for Switzerland, the French government shut down the 700-year-old Abbey of Melleray, a daughterhouse of Cîteaux in the Loire Val-ley. Although Dom Augustin and his exiled brothers could not have known it at the time, the story of their struggle to preserve the Trappist way of life would for years to come be linked not only to the remarkable comeback of the Abbey of Melleray, but also to the subsequent founding of its first American daughterhouse in the untamed hills of frontier Kentucky.

ABOVE: *The Abbey of La Trappe, where the Trappist Reform began.*

OPPOSITE: *A church bell left by the first Trappists in America in 1803.*

ON the ROAD:
KENTUCKY'S FIRST TRAPPISTS
and CATHOLIC PIONEERS
1785-1847

THEY SAY TENACITY IS A CISTERCIAN TRAIT. No less an authority than Thomas Merton claimed it as a defining characteristic in his 1949 history of the order, *The Waters of Siloe*. Generally speaking, Merton was right, of course. But the exception that proves his rule arrived in Kentucky, exhausted and malnourished, in the autumn of 1805.

It was, indeed, an exceptional band of French Trappists from the Abbey of La Valsainte who pulled into port at Louisville that September. They had begun their trip in Pennsylvania, at a place called Pigeon Hill, where they briefly considered founding a monastery – what could have been the first permanent Trappist foundation in America – on a farm 50 miles outside of Baltimore.

There were some 20 of them in the party: monks and lay brothers and boys who belonged to the community's Third Order. They had started out in July in covered wagons, crossing the Appalachians at a respectable pace, waking in the middle of the night to chant together as they made their way slowly through wooded valleys and mountain passes. At the Monongahela River, they bought two flatboats, loaded them with horses, baggage and food supplies, then climbed aboard. The river was low in places, and they frequently ran aground. At best, they covered 15 miles a day.

But they pushed on. At Pittsburgh, they bought bigger boats and headed down the Ohio River. At Cincinnati, they sold one boat to buy food. Another sank. A pair of the brothers were sent by land to Louisville with the horses, but most of the animals died on the way. When the single remaining flatboat finally reached Louisville, it was crammed with men and boys and whatever belongings were still in their possession. The men were tired and weak but determined not to

The Pioneer Years

1776: American Revolution begins.

1778: George Rogers Clark establishes base on Corn Island at Falls of the Ohio.

1785: First wave of Maryland Catholics arrives in Kentucky.

1787: Father Charles M. Whelan is first priest to settle in Kentucky.

1789: Father William de Rohan settles at hill still known as Rohan's Knob.

1794: Father Badin settles at Pottinger's Creek, 15 miles from Bardstown.

1800: Kentucky population passes 200,000.

1803: Louisiana Purchase.

1804: Lewis and Clark begin expedition.

1805: Father Charles Nerinckx, the Shakers and Valsainte Trappists arrive in Kentucky.

1806: Holy Roman Empire officially ends after 1,000 years.

1807: U.S. bans importation of slaves.

1808: Bardstown Diocese is formed.

1811: Flaget arrives in Kentucky after Trappists have moved on.

1818: Sisters of Loretto establish Gethsemani on land donated by Dants.

1847: The Loretto Sisters sell Gethsemani to Trappists of Melleray, France.

linger. Their destination was further south, in an area of central Kentucky that would later be known as the "The Catholic Holy Land" for its concentration of Catholic settlements. Near Bardstown, which was to become the seat of a new diocese in 1808, Father Stephen Badin, the first priest ordained in America, was waiting for them. Three priests in the Trappist community died soon after their arrival. Victims of illnesses they could not resist in their weakened condition, they were buried in the Holy Cross churchyard, where two other Trappist priests and three lay brothers were also laid to rest. Today a plaque at the site honors all eight men.

Clearly, these Trappists showed uncommon courage and remarkable perseverance for the entire length of their perilous cross-country journey. But when it came to a commitment to stay put on Kentucky soil, they exhibited anything but Cistercian tenacity. By the fall of 1809, they were gone.

Lured by what they believed were greener monastic pastures (and despite a generous neighbor's offer of 2,000 acres of free land on nearby Nolin Creek), the first Trappists in Kentucky abandoned their newfound home — the 800-acre settlement on Casey Creek with its 60 acres of cultivated farmland; the log-cabin monastery; the school on Pottinger's Creek; the sawmill; the thriving watchmaking business and the many friends and benefactors who wanted them to stay.

In 1808, floods devastated their crops, and a fire destroyed most of their library. That might have been good reason to move on, but well before those tragedies struck, the monks had begun building flatboats – the vehicles for their getaway in April 1809. No good reason was ever recorded for their decision to pull up roots and seek a new site for their foundation; at least not any reason compatible with Cistercian logic.

Brief though their stay was, these Valsainte monks played an important role in Gethsemani's history. Yes, their hasty departure left a sour taste in the mouths of some Kentuckians, including Fr. Badin, who couldn't understand why they were in such a rush to leave and who, presumably, was left to explain the unpaid debt on their land. But 40 years later, when a second party of French Trappists arrived in the same neck of the woods, these monks – from the Abbey of Melleray – were enthusiastically received by the people of Bardstown and its surrounding villages. In part, this was because some local Catholics had never forgotten, nor stopped talking about the quiet life and ancient rituals the Valsainte monks had introduced to the frontier wilderness.

To understand why the first Trappists did not stay put, it helps to know the history of that particular colony of monks. Valsainte, their motherhouse, was the Swiss monastery where the austere reformers of La Trappe had found refuge during the French Revolution. Dom Urban Guillet, the monk who led the Trappist expedition to America, was by all accounts more crusader than contemplative. In his defense, he had *not* experienced a conventional Cistercian upbringing.

Dom Urban (who was not really a "dom" at all since he never headed up an abbey) was the last professed novice at La Trappe before the Revolution. He followed

An 18th-century engraving of the Abbey of La Trappe.

Holy Cross Church, where eight monks from the first Trappist colony in Kentucky are buried.

the ardent reformer of that house, Dom Augustin de Lestrange, to Valsainte when the political climate became too dangerous to stay. There, as a young man, he endured extreme hardship and deprivation. Later he wandered Europe and Asia as a wartime refugee, sometimes making his treks on foot, often while sick or hungry. In 1803, after finally returning to Valsainte, Fr. Urban was told to lead a colony of men and boys to America and make a foundation there. By necessity, solitude and stability had taken a back seat to activity and travel in Fr. Urban's monastic education.

When Fr. Urban arrived in Baltimore, he was 36 years old. Whether by nature or by nurture, he was at that point consumed by a nomadic restlessness and a missionary's appetite for adventure. Born of a Creole mother and French father at Nantes, he has been variously described as an optimist, a naif and (by Merton) a scoutmaster. No one ever accused him of being too contemplative. He was the instigator of Valsainte's Third Order, which offered a free education to

40

young men without obligating them to join the community. This practice, hardly compatible with Cistercian simplicity, was later terminated.

Before coming to Kentucky, Fr. Urban spent two years with his monks at Pigeon Hill, living in a spacious farm house on land owned by a friend of the Sulpician fathers, who had taken the Trappists under wing. But, fearing the boys in the community might be distracted by the big-city enticements of nearby Baltimore, Fr. Urban soon was seeking a more isolated location for his foundation.

The out-of-the-way place he ultimately chose was Kentucky; he may have been motivated by first-hand reports of the untamed frontier passed on to him by travelers. In any case, Fr. Urban and two companions – one of whom was an interpreter – went ahead to scout a suitable site for a monastery. By July 1805, the rest of the community was on its way to join them on land leased to them near Fr. Badin's Holy Cross Church. But Fr. Urban wanted to own land, not rent it. The following summer, he wrote to the bishop of Quebec about his hope of landing the larger Casey Creek farm some 30 miles from where they were.

With characteristic optimism, he wrote: "I have found a piece of land just right for a monastery but they are asking $4,000, and I have only $4."

That winter, to Bishop Carroll back in Maryland, Fr. Urban described the monks' new home enthusiastically: "We will be able to have on our land several mills, ponds for fish, a large number of livestock and horses, some rice, sugar, grain of all kinds, as well as cotton. Water, wood, stone to build; in a word, all that is most necessary except iron."

Fr. Urban got the land he wanted, buying it with money he borrowed from a local supporter. His monks moved to Casey Creek farm. The journey took six days, largely because a path had to be cleared through 18 miles of forest. Fr. Urban, whose rheumatism was acting up, and four monks who were either too old or too sick to make the trek stayed behind with some of the Third Order boys. At the site, the monks set up temporary quarters in huts on the property and immediately began building a mill. This seemed to be the fulfillment of Fr. Urban's dream. And yet, in less than two years, he and his monks were on the road again.

WHEN THOSE FIRST TRAPPISTS LEFT KENTUCKY FOR good in October 1809, they were far from finished with their wandering. They stopped briefly at Florrisant, Missouri, where local citizens offered to help them make a foundation; then moved on to Cahokia, Illinois, near what is now East St. Louis. As it turned out, the curious low mounds surrounding that settlement were actually Indian graves, and the polluted waters of its creek led to an outbreak of typhoid at the monastery.

Though hardly in keeping with the spirit of stability, Fr. Urban's decision to keep moving west reflected the general mood of the country at the time. Meriwether Lewis and William Clark had recently launched their historic expedition across the Mississippi River and up the Missouri into the newly acquired Louisiana Territory. Their explorations were inspiring a national mythology.

But Fr. Urban's westward wandering ended abruptly in 1813. Having survived earthquakes and winter freezes at their Illinois settlement, the Trappists at Cahokia now found themselves summoned to the island of Manhattan. Dom Augustin had found what he thought was the perfect place for a foundation.

The Valsainte monks lived briefly on an estate where St. Patrick's Cathedral now stands, and then – was anyone surprised? – they moved on. The political climate back home was changing. France was once again a safe place for monks. After a decade of wandering through America, the Trappists returned to France in 1814, leaving behind both their dream of an American foundation and the Kentucky Catholics with whom they had once shared it.

SETTLING the HOLY LAND:
THE CATHOLIC PIONEERS of
KENTUCKY

Father Stephen Badin, the first priest ordained in America.

THE FIRST COLONY OF CATHOLIC SETTLERS CAME TO Kentucky from Maryland in 1785, making its home that summer at Pottinger's Creek. The group, as a whole, was made up of fiercely independent men and women. In his book, *An American Holy Land*, Kentucky historian Father Clyde Crews calls them "survivors who . . . knew how to suffer and to serve and to celebrate." Survival in those days required a certain wiliness, and they had that, too. They traveled to Kentucky as a group of families, so the story goes, because they knew it would enhance their chances of snaring a priest. It was not a bad strategy.

The first priest to join them in the Nelson County wilderness was Charles M. Whelan, a middle-aged Capuchin friar from New York who arrived in 1787 at the invitation of John Carroll, the first bishop of the United States. But before long a salary dispute landed Fr. Whelan and his flock in court, battling over the legality of his contract. Within three years he was back east, where he died in 1806.

The second priest to settle in Kentucky was William

de Rohan who joined the Pottinger's Creek colony the fall that Fr. Whelan left. His legacy is legend in Nelson County. At the foot of a hill that people still refer to as Rohan's Knob, he built the commonwealth's first Catholic church, Holy Cross. But he, too, had his problems: chronic alcoholism took its toll. Although Father de Rohan taught sporadically in Kentucky for another 30 years, his work as a parish priest was over by 1793.

The man who turned things around for the fledgling settlement was Stephen Badin, the priest who was later to play host to Kentucky's first Trappists. An exile of the French Revolution, Father Badin became the first priest ordained in America on May 23, 1793. A few months later, he left Baltimore where he had been ordained, and made his way to Kentucky, where he settled at Pottinger's Creek.

In 1805, the year the Trappists arrived, Fr. Badin published a book, *The Principles of Roman Catholics*, which included a section debunking rumors about American Catholics, in particular the allegation that

Washington Cy, Kentucky — viz.

Memorandum of an agreement entered into this twenty first of January in the year of our Lord eighteen hundred and eight between the Revd Stephen Theodore Badin & Joseph Dant both of the County and State aforesaid.

Joseph Dant, on the consideration to be mentioned below, does hereby Sell unto S. T. Badin the plantation devised and willed unto him by his father John Baptist Dant, laying on the waters of Pottingers Creek; & the said S. T. Badin shall erect or cause to be erected thereon a monastery or School for the female youth, to be taught greading, writing & the elements of the christian religion. In witness whereof the contracting parties have hereunto set their hands & seals

In presence of   Joseph Dant

James Dant   Stephen Theodore Badin
Stephen Elliott.
Thomas Shiercliff

*Legal document refering to
land at Pottinger's Creek, near the
present site of the Abbey of Gethsemani, transferred
from the Dant family to Father Badin in 1808.*

ABOVE: *An 1816 etching by a Belgian artist, depicting the settlement on Hardin's Creek where the Sisters of Loretto established their motherhouse.* RIGHT: *Bishop Benedict Joseph Flaget, the first bishop of the diocese of Bardstown, and pages from a diary he kept.* OPPOSITE: *Father Charles Nerinckx, the Belgian priest who arrived in Kentucky in 1805, and the cabin where he first lived.*

inckx formulated a religious rule for a community of women. In 1812, that rule became the basis of The Sisters of Loretto, founded by Rhodes and her friends. Wishing to help the new community, Dant offered them his farm and the house that incorporated St. Barbara's chapel. In March 1818, six Loretto sisters opened a boarding school there and named it "Gethsemani." From the start, it flourished.

Some 25 years later, the enrollment had grown to 100 pupils, many of them orphans. Nevertheless, by 1847, the Sisters of Loretto had decided to sell the Dant property, which included a farm, several buildings and a grist mill. And who turned up to buy it? None else but the French monks of the Abbey of Melleray, the second colony of Trappists to seek a home in Kentucky. The monks paid $5,000 for the old Dant property, kept the name that the Sisters of Loretto had given it and made their foundation there in 1848. One-hundred-fifty years later, the monks of Gethsemani are still there.

they could not be loyal to both their government and their church. That same year, a Shaker community settled at Pleasant Hill, Kentucky, and the Dominicans made their home near Springfield. Religious life was prospering in the backwoods of Kentucky.

CHARLES NERINCKX, A BELGIAN PRIEST WHO WOULD play an indirect, but crucial role in Gethsemani's early history, also arrived in 1805. The story of that fateful connection spans nearly four decades and involves the foundation of the first religious community in Kentucky, the Sisters of Loretto at the Foot of the Cross. From letters of the era, it appears that soon after his arrival, Fr. Nerinckx began attending Masses that were held regularly at the Nelson County home of James Dant and his wife. The room where they worshiped came to be known as St. Barbara's Chapel.

A few years later, at the request of Dant's young cousin, Mary Rhodes, and two of her friends, Fr. Ner-

THE STORY OF KENTUCKY'S EARLY CATHOLICS WOULD not be complete without mention of Benedict Joseph Flaget, the first bishop of the diocese of Bardstown. He never knew any of the monks in that first Trappist colony. By the time he arrived in Kentucky in 1811, they had already abandoned their Casey Creek monastery.

But Bishop Flaget had a long, eventful tenure and was still presiding over the diocese in 1848 when the Trappists of Melleray pulled into port at Louisville. With open arms, the 86-year-old bishop, himself a native of France, welcomed the weary monks to his cathedral where they rested several days before heading for Gethsemani, their new Kentucky home.

The Martinique Letters:
An Historic Sidetrip Along the Road to Gethsemani

In the 1840s, in the French colony of Martinique, roughly 72,000 slaves performed nearly all the manual labor and plantation work for the island's free population, which numbered about 33,000.

This troubled French officials for two reasons. They knew slavery's days were numbered. And they sensed that when emancipation came, it would create havoc for the lopsided economies of their colonial islands, including Martinique. Who would work the sugar cane plantations, for example? The French feared that freed slaves would no longer want the jobs they once had been forced to perform. And who could blame them?

The only way to solve the problem, the French believed, was to somehow make manual labor in the fields seem respectable rather than demeaning. What they needed, they decided, was to get free white men into the fields, working at the same jobs the slaves had held. More than anything else could, this would convey the message that manual labor was a worthy calling and not just the occupation of slaves.

But what respectable group of white men, they wondered, would willingly perform such menial tasks?

Their answer came without hesitation: Monks, of course.

So they hatched a plot. The government would encourage Trappists to make a foundation in Martinique. The monks would work their fields as was their custom wherever they lived. And the newly liberated slaves? They would be so inspired by the industrious monks that they would continue to perform the plantation chores that the French colonials needed done.

Despite the plan's patronizing attitude toward slaves and monks alike, French officials immediately set out to make it happen. Thanks to Gethsemani's Father Chrysogonus Waddell and his research on this subject, the story of this curious episode is well documented.

In 1846, a French bureaucrat wrote a confidential memorandum outlining the Trappist "Solution:"

We know that by reason of their Rule, this Order is devoted exclusively to agricultural work. . . . When (the black population) has before its eyes the permanent sight of the holy and laborious way of life of the Trappists, when they see day after day these holy men, whose whole life strikes them with admiration and respect, cultivating the land with their hands, using the hoe and the plow, in a word, taking precisely for its lot the occupation nowadays reserved for slaves, there can be no doubt but that the free Black will end by effecting a complete revolution of his thinking. Work now shared by God's elect . . . will no longer be able to be in his eyes something degrading and unworthy of a free man. His prejudice will vanish. This will be the infallible result.

Wasting no time, the head of the colonial office wrote the Secretary of Navy, endorsing the plan:

There can be no doubt but that such an example given by men consecrated to God, and wearing the monastic habit, would exercise the most salutary influence. . . . Should the Secretary approve this line of thought, overtures could be made officially, first of all to the Superior of the Trappists.

A meeting at La Grande Trappe was quickly arranged. Representing the Trappists were Dom Maxime of the Abbey of Melleray and Dom Hercelin, abbot of La Trappe and vicar general. Two Catholic government officials also attended. As Fr. Chrysogonus notes in his commentary on the Martinique letters, organized religion was experiencing a comeback in France at the time. Melleray was an example of this rebirth of religious liberty and fervor. Where 50 years earlier there had been an empty monastery, shut down by the government for 25 years, there now was a thriving community of more than 150 choir monks and lay brothers.

But there were wrinkles in the fabric of that spiri-

46

AT WORK IN THE FIELD.

tual revival. For example, the only legal rights a monastery such as Melleray could claim at the time were those guaranteed to any profit-sharing organization covered by the civil code. Melleray, Fr. Chrysogonus notes, was officially nothing more than a "corporation of farm workers, who only accidentally happened to get together for religious exercises." Freedom of religion was not part of the French civil code. It behooved a monastery not to rock the bureaucratic boat.

With all this in mind, the Trappists accepted the government's invitation to consider a foundation in Martinique. In the fall of 1846, Trappist scouts were sent to the island to check out the proposed site, the St. Jacques sugar cane plantation. That winter, Father Eutropius Proust of the Abbey of Melleray, the monk chosen to be superior of the foundation, wrote a letter to friends describing why Trappists would consider such an enterprise: "The purpose . . . is to bring labor back into honor, to inspire a taste for it in all classes and thus to obtain liberty for these wretched slaves whose condition resembles that of domestic animals."

The following March, the monks made their official report to the government. They duly noted the dangers rampant in Martinique, from the blistering tropical climate and occasionally devastating earthquakes to the tragic social and moral consequences of state-sanctioned slavery. On the other hand, they were enthusiastic about "the chance to raise from bondage a race kept in degradation by several centuries of slavery." However, they believed that liberation had to come in stages, not all at once. Otherwise, they concluded, chaos would reign.

La Trappe's Dom Hercelin, who was in Africa when the report was submitted, wrote to the Secretary of the Navy upon his return, adding several stipulations of his own. The Secretary acceded to most of them but made it clear the Trappists would be expected to pay for their property. He offered a government subsidy to cover part of the expense and a long-term loan for the rest. The proposed monastery and its surrounding 1,000 acres were also described in great detail, right down to the nine-foot enclosure wall and the 150-foot facade. This was clearly a plan the government was ready to execute.

At the start of 1848, all that remained was for both parties to sign the agreement. But before that happened, the French government fell, bringing down with it the Trappists' plans for a monastery in Martinique.

A month after the fall of Louis Philippe's government, Fr. Eutropius Proust of the Abbey of Melleray managed to meet in person with the new Undersecretary of State, a Mr. Schelcher. Fr. Eutropius sensed from the conversation that the new government, which supported immediate emancipation of slaves but was less certain about the rights of religious, was not keen on having a monastic order in charge of the process in Martinique — especially not one that wanted to liberate the slaves by stages. The plan for a foundation there was dropped.

But that certainly was not the only bad news Fr. Eutropius gleaned from their conversation. Schelcher admitted to him he was not sure "what would be the future of religious bodies" under the new regime. It was an unsettling comment, and one that Fr. Eutropius shared with Dom Maxime when he returned to Melleray.

That was March 1848. Seven months later, Dom Maxime sent Fr. Eutropius and 43 of his Melleray brothers across the Atlantic to the New World. They settled at a place called Gethsemani in a country, like Martinique, where slavery's days were numbered. This time, however, they made their foundation without the aid of any government and with no strings attached.

A FINAL WORD on the FIRST TRAPPISTS

In real life, most stories don't end neatly. There's rarely a place to point and say, "This is the ending." Plots overlap. Characters enter and leave at will.

And so it was with the Trappists of Valsainte. When they sailed from New York back to France in the fall of 1814, the story of their North American journey was, in one sense, only beginning.

It all goes back to a certain French Trappist, Father Vincent de Paul Merle, who had joined forces with Fr. Urban and Dom Augustin during their last days in New York. When the others set sail for France, Fr. Vincent stayed behind with some lay brothers to tie up the community's loose ends.

The following May, their work complete, Fr. Vincent and his brothers were in Halifax, Nova Scotia, ready to sail on the next ship home. But, due to some last-minute confusion over the departure time of their ship, Fr. Vincent was left behind.

Father Vincent de Paul Merle,
founder of Petit Clairvaux.

For Fr. Vincent, this was a mixed blessing. Since he had not approved of the decision to leave North America in the first place, he did not consider it a tragedy to be stranded there. On the other hand, what was he to do next – a Trappist alone in a foreign country? Eager to make the most of the situation, he first hammered out a deal with Bishop Plessis of Quebec to help with his Halifax parishes, then obtained permission from Dom Augustin to attempt a foundation in the area.

Like Fr. Urban, Fr. Vincent had an unconventional Cistercian upbringing. He, too, had been buffeted about during the Revolutionary years in France and, before meeting up with his abbot in New York, had spent sev-

eral years trying unsuccessfully to make foundations in Pennsylvania and Maryland. None had succeeded, but that had not diminished his missionary zeal.

His luck turned in Nova Scotia. There, in a wooded valley on a 300-acre tract a half-mile from the coast, near a settlement known as Big Tracadie, he founded the monastery of Petit Clairvaux in 1825.

But this is still not the end of the story.

Nearly 70 years later, on October 4, 1892, a devastating fire reduced Petit Clairvaux to a brick shell. A second fire in 1896 thwarted the community's attempts to rebuild. Without adequate living quarters or farm buildings, the community that Fr. Vincent had founded now joined forces temporarily with the Trappists of Our Lady of the Lake, near Montreal. In August 1900, the Petit Clairvaux community moved to Rhode Island and took a new name, Our Lady of the Valley.

In 1913, beset by agricultural problems and a shortage of monks, Our Lady of the Valley was temporarily turned over to the Abbey of Gethsemani as an adopted daughterhouse. However, once on its feet again, the monastery flourished, and by the 1940s had grown large and prosperous enough to make its own foundation in New Mexico.

Then, in 1950, fire destroyed Our Lady of the Valley just as it had devastated Petit Clairvaux before it. The monks built a new monastery in Spencer, Massachusetts, known as St. Joseph's Abbey, where the community resides today.

50

Dom Eutropius Proust:
America's Proto-Abbot
1848-1859

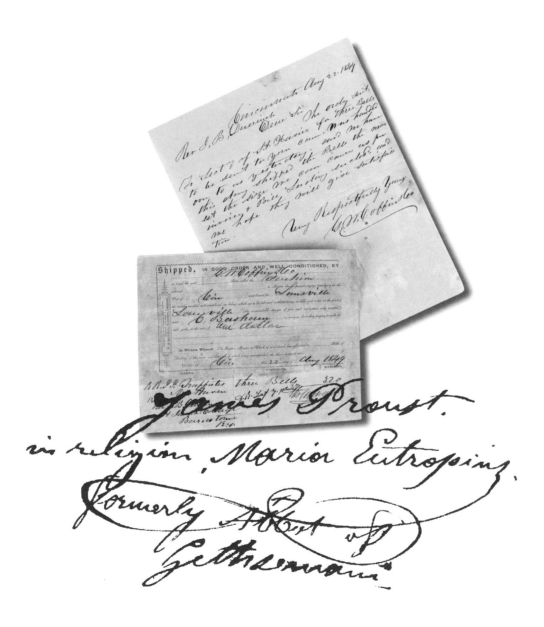

The Abbey of Melleray, Gethsemani's motherhouse in France, at the crossroads
where the monks leaving for America separated from their brothers.

LEAVING HOME

KNOWING WHERE YOU COME FROM IS A VALUABLE piece of information to have on the journey to wherever it is you are going. Cistercian monks figured this out long ago. Beginning with the founding of Citeaux, they went to great lengths to ensure that the story of each new house – how it came to be – was never forgotten. As new foundations were made, their stories were recorded. From generation to generation, details rich in significance were passed on, sometimes by mouth but usually on paper.

The monks of Gethsemani are no exception to this Cistercian storytelling tradition. In the archives of the monastery, there are many versions of the birth of their abbey. Some are hand-written and date from the time of the foundation. Others are neatly typed on yellowed pages. They can be found stuffed in dusty manila folders and carefully arranged in treated envelopes. Some accounts are published in books written by distinguished authors. Some show up in letters. Annals exist, and official histories. So do popular accounts, written for magazines and newspapers.

Each time the story of the founding of Gethsemani is retold, by scholar or journalist or casual visitor, a new perspective develops, fresh insights reveal themselves.

Gethsemani's story begins inauspiciously, as the most memorable stories always do. The weather does not cooperate: it's cold, damp and dark as the Trappist party of 44 men and boys leaves the French Abbey of Melleray on foot. Danger, both political and physical, threatens every step of the way. The monks get separated, lose their luggage, come up short of cash. But always they make their destination. God's plan – not man's – operates here.

Because it is an archetypal story of origins, time and personalities tend to collapse within it. Events that occurred 150 years ago take on shades of the present. It is as if the Trappist who runs the computers at the abbey today and the Trappist who left Melleray on foot in October of 1848 are one and the same monk.

There is a belief among Jews that every Jew – past, present and future – was there, on Mount Sinai, the day that Moses received God's law. The spiritual bloodline that binds one Jew to another renders time and space irrelevant, they say. All are one on the mountain: ancient prophet of Israel, Medieval rabbi and 21st-century American Jew.

This same thing could be said of the French Trappists who founded Gethsemani and the American Trappists who live there today. Their stories are really one story, and this is where it begins.

MONKS GOING on a JOURNEY:
THE BIRTH of GETHSEMANI

WELL BEFORE FRENCH POLITICS PUT AN END TO Melleray's plans for a foundation in Martinique, Dom Maxime had two of his monks scouting Kentucky for land suitable for a Trappist monastery. Father Paulinus, the prior of Melleray, and Father Paul, a choir monk, made the trip in 1847, months before the fall of the government of Louis Philippe.

The first stop on their expedition was Louisville, where Bishop Flaget greeted them warmly and assigned them a personal guide. The three men immediately headed for Nelson County, to look for land in the same neighborhood where decades earlier the Trappists of Valsainte had made a temporary home. Fr. Paulinus quickly negotiated a deal with the Sisters of Loretto for the land and buildings already known as Gethsemani.

Most written versions of this story describe the property as lying "in the shadow" of Rohan's Knob, which was of course the burial site of the first eight Valsainte Trappists to die in Kentucky. Whether or not Fr. Paulinus chose the Loretto tract because of its physical proximity to that earlier attempt at a foundation, we can't be sure. But it is easy to imagine the psychological appeal of such a connection. In a country whose customs and terrain were wildly unfamiliar, there must have

been some comfort in knowing a Trappist presence was already a part of the neighborhood and its lore.

Once Fr. Paulinus returned home with the good news of his land deal, Melleray's plans for the Gethsemani foundation began to take shape. The Loretto property would cost $5,000, and it would include some 1,500 acres of farm and woodland as well as a number of buildings, some in poor repair. By mid-October, according to Melleray records, a visiting priest from Mississippi was making promises to Dom Maxime that he would keep in touch with the delegation once it arrived.

It is clear from all accounts that the making of this foundation was a bittersweet proposition. On one hand, there was great excitement and joy in organizing a colony that, if all went as hoped, would become the first permanent Trappist foundation in America. On the other hand, it meant dividing a community, abdicating national allegiances, embarking on an unpredictable journey.

ON OCTOBER 26, 1848, THE COMMUNITY WOKE TO A steady cold rain. At about 7 a.m., the 44 who would be leaving Melleray that day changed into street clothes for the trip. Their leader was Fr. Eutropius Proust, a native

This Indenture made and entered into this the 14th day of August 1850. Between the Corporation of the Loretto Literary and Benevolent Female Institution of Marion County and Commonwealth of Kentucky of the one part and The Fathers Eutropius Proust, Paulinas Sarante, Eutymius Leverton, and Emmanuel LeRoy in Trust for the Community of La Trappe and of the County Nelson and State aforesaid Witnesseth. That the Party of the First part for and in Consideration of the sum of five thousand Dollars in hand paid the receipt whereof is hereby acknowledged hath Granted bargained and Sold and by these presents doth Grant Bargain Sell and Convey unto the Party of the Second part for the purpose specified above all that tract of Land lying on Pottengers Creek and its tributaries, in Nelson County and known by the Name of Gethsemani it being the Lands deeded by James David To Bishop Flaget and the Lands deeded by Revd Robt Byrne to The Corporation of the Loretto Literary and benevolent Female Institution To which deeds reference is made for boundary Containing Eleven Hundred and Sixteen 73/4 acres be the Same more or less. To have and to hold the Land hereby Conveyed with the appurtenances unto the said Party of the Second part and their Successors forever and the said Party of the first part by the Trustees of the Corporation for themselves and their Successors the aforesaid

ABOVE: *The Abbey of Melleray as it looks today.*
LEFT: *The original deed for the property called "Gethsemani," owned by the Sisters of Loretto and purchased by the French Trappists.*

of the Vendee region of France who had entered Melleray only four years earlier. At 39, he was, according to Merton's description of him in *The Waters of Siloe,* "a thin, wiry, intense little man . . . full of ideals."

A moving account of that last morning at Melleray is found in the abbey's register. Everyone gathered in the church, according to this eyewitness account. Those who were staying took seats in the upper choir stalls; those leaving assembled in the lower ones. Melleray's church, which still stands today, was built in the 12th century. Most of the monastery's current buildings came centuries later, as replacements or additions to structures that were ravaged either by war or by time. They reflect various architectural schools and styles. But the early

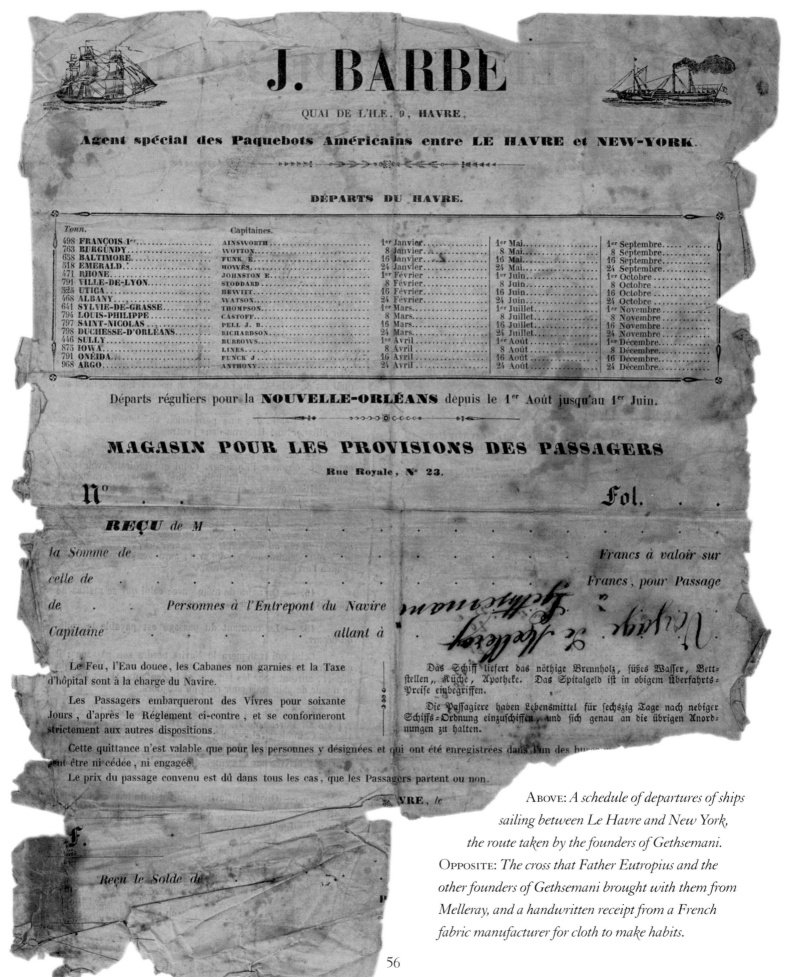

J. BARBE

QUAI DE L'ILE, 9, HAVRE,

Agent spécial des Paquebots Américains entre LE HAVRE et NEW-YORK.

DÉPARTS DU HAVRE.

Tonn.		Capitaines.			
498	FRANÇOIS 1er	AINSWORTH	1er Janvier	1er Mai	1er Septembre
763	BURGUNDY	WOTTON	8 Janvier	8 Mai	8 Septembre
658	BALTIMORE	FUNK E.	16 Janvier	16 Mai	16 Septembre
518	EMERALD	HOWES	24 Janvier	24 Mai	24 Septembre
471	RHONE	JOHNSTON E.	1er Février	1er Juin	1er Octobre
791	VILLE-DE-LYON	STODDARD	8 Février	8 Juin	8 Octobre
525	UTICA	HEWITT	16 Février	16 Juin	16 Octobre
468	ALBANY	WATSON	24 Février	24 Juin	24 Octobre
641	SYLVIE-DE-GRASSE	THOMPSON	1er Mars	1er Juillet	1er Novembre
794	LOUIS-PHILIPPE	CASTOFF	8 Mars	8 Juillet	8 Novembre
797	SAINT-NICOLAS	PELL J. B.	16 Mars	16 Juillet	16 Novembre
798	DUCHESSE-D'ORLÉANS	RICHARDSON	24 Mars	24 Juillet	24 Novembre
446	SULLY	BURROWS	1er Avril	1er Août	1er Décembre
875	IOWA	LINES	8 Avril	8 Août	8 Décembre
791	ONÉIDA	FUNCK J	16 Avril	16 Août	16 Décembre
968	ARGO	ANTHONY	24 Avril	24 Août	24 Décembre

Départs réguliers pour la **NOUVELLE-ORLÉANS** depuis le 1er Août jusqu'au 1er Juin.

MAGASIN POUR LES PROVISIONS DES PASSAGERS

Rue Royale, N° 23.

N°   Fol.

REÇU de M

la Somme de   Francs à valoir sur

celle de   Francs, pour Passage

de   Personnes à l'Entrepont du Navire

Capitaine   allant à

Le Feu, l'Eau douce, les Cabanes non garnies et la Taxe d'hôpital sont à la charge du Navire.

Les Passagers embarqueront des Vivres pour soixante Jours, d'après le Réglement ci-contre, et se conformeront strictement aux autres dispositions.

Cette quittance n'est valable que pour les personnes y désignées et qui ont été enregistrées dans l'un des bureaux peut être ni cédée, ni engagée.

Le prix du passage convenu est dû dans tous les cas, que les Passagers partent ou non.

Das Schiff liefert das nöthige Brennholz, süßes Wasser, Bett-stellen, Küche, Apotheke. Das Spitalgeld ist in obigem Überfahrts-Preise einbegriffen.

Die Passagiere haben Lebensmittel für sechszig Tage nach nebiger Schiffs-Ordnung einzuschiffen, und sich genau an die übrigen Anord-nungen zu halten.

VRE, le

F.

Reçu le Solde de

ABOVE: *A schedule of departures of ships sailing between Le Havre and New York, the route taken by the founders of Gethsemani.*
OPPOSITE: *The cross that Father Eutropius and the other founders of Gethsemani brought with them from Melleray, and a handwritten receipt from a French fabric manufacturer for cloth to make habits.*

Cistercian ideals of simplicity and serenity are reflected in the stark gracefulness of the Melleray church, which has changed little over its nearly 900 years as a place of quiet worship.

It was from the church's main altar that Dom Maxime launched the morning's long good-bye. He began with a reading of a traditional prayer for "monks going on a journey." A cantor then chanted a song that was picked up by the two choirs and sung, according to our eyewitness, in a tone that was both "grave and animated." A copy had been made of the cross that had been carried by Dom Augustin as he led the monks of La Trappe on their flight from France to La Valsainte, Switzerland. Now the original and the copy were fastened together. Dom Maxime said a solemn blessing over both. When two monks started chanting the Litany of the Blessed Virgin, everyone rose, and the farewell procession began.

At the head of the cortege, one monk carried holy water, another had the incense; the cross bearer followed between two acolytes. The Gethsemani colony came next: choir monks wearing cowls over their street clothes, lay brothers covered in cloaks. The abbot walked in the middle, his ivory crosier in hand, as the rest of the community fell in behind him. They left the church by the large front door, then re-entered the monastic enclosure by the main gate. In silence, they passed the exterior wall of the monastery and stopped at the edge of a wood.

There the abbot separated the two crosses, handing one to Fr. Eutropius to carry with him for the next two months as he and his monks made their way to America.

"Then took place the most touching spectacle conceivable," says our reporter in the Melleray register. Those who would not be leaving the monastery formed two long lines, ranking themselves according to seniority. The Gethsemani travelers then walked down those lines, one by one, offering a last kiss of peace to their brothers. "Tears flowed from all eyes," says our author. "There was a lump in every throat. . . . On all sides only the signs of deepest grief were to be seen."

Gethsemani's founders are frequently depicted as robust, hardy villagers, the sons of sturdy farmers and resourceful fishermen in the Vendee. But here we get a picture of a different side of these men. If the physical demands of making a foundation would tax their bodies and exhaust their physical reserves, it's clear from this passage that there was an emotional toll as well. These 44 Trappists – all but two of whom were French citizens – were surrendering not only their spiritual home, the monastery they had vowed never to leave; they were giving up their motherland as well, their native tongue, their culture, everything and everyone they had ever known and loved.

When the parting words had been said, Dom Maxime boarded a carriage to accompany the colony as far as Ancenis. Two other carriages transported baggage and several monks deemed too weak to make the 17-mile trek. Everyone else in the party started down the muddy road on foot, each one carrying two blankets for sleeping on the journey.

At Ancenis, a small town on the bank of the Loire River, the troupe arrived late in the day, worn out and hungry. They had not stopped to eat along the way. Fortunately, a wealthy Catholic patron opened her home to them, and the local priest gave them permission to use his church for Compline, the choral office that comes at the end of day. Word spread quickly of this rare opportunity to hear Trappists sing the *Salve Regina*, the haunting closing hymn of Compline. The residents of Ancenis packed the church, and afterwards surrounded the Trappists as they hurried to the wharf to board their steamboat. There was much confusion as the crowd pushed and shoved around them.

Several times, they were forced to stop and count heads to make sure no one had been lost in the shuffle. They were warned of the possibility of political riots in Paris, but they never dreamed that at Ancenis their plans would be jeopardized by overzealous worshippers. At some point, it began to rain again, and the crowd ran for cover – a timely intervention for which the monks thanked God. When they finally reached the harbor, Fr. Eutropius called roll one last time; they had lost no one.

They were less successful, however, keeping track of their property. At Ancenis, Fr. Eutropius learned that their baggage was lost, their provisions misplaced and an expected loan of 8,000 francs had failed to materialize. At each stop along the way – and there were plenty – he worked on solving these problems. At Tours, where they switched to rail travel, at Orleans where they changed trains, and at Paris, Fr. Eutropius asked railroad officials about the missing 15,000 pounds of baggage and supplies. He received many promises from kind and concerned bureaucrats – but no baggage.

Three days before their ship was to sail from Le Havre, he was still trying to track it down. He decided to return to Paris where, at the last possible moment, the baggage did indeed turn up. However, it was at the wrong station. That evening, Fr. Eutropius hired three teamsters to move the baggage across town. He knew there was not sufficient time to check it through Paris customs, as the law required, so he paid the movers a few extra francs to drive around the walls of the city. The tactic worked: they made it to the station just in time.

Back at Le Havre, safe and sound, Fr. Eutropius made sure nothing was left on the wharf as the community boarded the *Brunswick*, an 800-ton sailing vessel. The Trappist community who gathered in the steerage section of the ship that day was a diverse and talented crew. Among their numbers were farmers and bookkeepers, three metal workers, a bee-keeper, a woodworker, a turner, three blacksmiths, a mechanic, a harness maker, a bookbinder, two cobblers, two carpenters, two bakers, a miller, a weaver, a barber, two stone-cutters, a painter, a cook, a mason, a nailsmith, a carder, a tinsmith, a cabinet maker, a sculptor, a physician and several with special skills in gardening, geometry, mathematics and surveying.

In the steerage section, which they had arranged to have all to themselves, the monks created a makeshift monastery. Among the items included in that 15,000 pounds of baggage that Fr. Eutropius was so intent on finding before they sailed were ovens and cookware. By the time the Trappists were ready for their first meal at sea, the kitchen they had improvised in the belly of the ship was serving up fresh baked bread and hot soup.

In New Orleans, having lost one of their number at sea, the remaining 43 founders of Gethsemani boarded the steamboat "Martha Washington" for Louisville.

Not every party that sailed on the *Brunswick* had prepared so well for the journey. In the end, the Gethsemani founders shared their meals regularly with others on board.

And it was a curious crowd that sailed with them, one that reflected the major social movements of the day. There were some 60 German immigrants, some of whom may have been lured by tales of that year's California Gold Rush.

More interesting, perhaps, to the monks was the band of 80 men, women and children who were on their way to Texas to set up a commune based on the doctrines of their leader, Etienne Cabet. The group was one of many utopian communities that grew out of the

52 1849.

Session IV.

Dans le dernier Chapitre Général de 1848, le R. P. Maxime, Abbé de Melleray avait demandé et obtenu l'autorisation de s'entendre avec le R.H. Vicaire Général pour mener à bonne fin un projet de fondation dans les États-unis d'Amérique.

Cette fondation a été faite. Nous avons au milieu de nous le R. P. Eutrope, Prieur titulaire de ce monastère.

Il nous donne des détails pleins d'intérêt sur le voyage des quarante religieux qu'il a emmenés avec lui de leur installation dans le Kentuki; on l'appelle Notre Dame de la Trappe de Gethsémani. La Colonie, partie de Melleray le 24 Octobre 1848, est arrivée à Gethsémanie le 21 Décembre.

Dans cette même Session, le R. P. Dom Bruno Abbé de Mont-Melleray en Irlande, nous fait part de l'établissement qu'il vient de fonder dans les États d'Iowa (États unis.) Il y a déjà installé six religieux; trente-quatre très n'attendent que son retour pour aller compléter la communauté. Le Chapitre Général y donne son adhésion. Ce sera le monastère de N.D. de la Trappe de la Nouvelle Melleray.

Session V

Il avait été question, dans une précédente session, d'un projet de fondation de religieuses de la Trappe de Ste Catherine dans le Diocèse de Vannes. On a demandé si Dom

In 1849, the General Chapter of the Order authorized the foundation at Gethsemani.

When their ship pulled into the port of New Orleans on Dec. 11, the Gethsemani colonists boarded the steamboat *Martha Washington* for the last leg of their trip to Louisville. The journey upriver took 10 days, and it was not nearly so comfortable or civilized as the high-seas portion of their voyage. The New World

European revolutions of that era. The Oneida community, for example, was founded earlier that year. There were similarities between the two groups on board the *Brunswick* that autumn, in terms of communal lifestyle, but the utopians were strictly non-religious. In fact, while at sea, they voted to forbid participation in the Trappists' Mass by any member of the group. Otherwise, the story goes, the two groups got along fine.

Into the midst of what was for the Trappists a mostly untroubled trip, sorrow did find its way. One of the monks, a 70-year-old Italian who had been a Christian Brother before entering Melleray, died aboard ship. Father Benezet was given a burial at sea.

proved immediately to be a rougher, tougher place to negotiate. On board the *Martha Washington,* the Trappists were hard put to keep a claim on their own straw mattresses, so desperate were some of their fellow passengers for a decent place to sleep. They surely must have been longing for a monastery to call their home by the time they pulled into the Falls of the Ohio the week before Christmas.

BUT THERE WAS ANOTHER DELAY AT THE FALLS, ENOUGH of one to prompt Fr. Eutropius to leave the ship on his own and hike the three miles or so into the city. He walked straight to Bishop Flaget's residence to let him know his Trappist foundation had arrived. It is often noted in historical accounts that Bishop Flaget was overcome with emotion at the sight of the weary French priest. The bishop was old, his health failing by then; he was to die within a few years. This encounter with the Trappist superior was one he had long anticipated, and perhaps secretly feared would never take place.

By the time the rest of the community made it to town, Bishop Flaget and Fr. Eutropius had agreed that the men should rest at the cathedral for a few days before setting off for Nelson County. There was work to be done in the interim; they needed to secure wagons and supplies for the 50-mile trip to Gethsemani.

It rained hard the day they left, an icy downpour that drenched the monks and ravaged the roads their three wagons had to travel. The terrain from Louisville to Bardstown rolled and curled into valleys and bottomlands and sometimes rose for miles on end, fatiguing the horses but providing impressive views of the surrounding countryside. It was an awesome route for the eyes to take in, but to the wayfarer attempting to traverse it, it was a formidable course, even in the best weather. In this case, mud oozed up the wagon wheels, threatening to mire the caravan and delay the trip.

After dark, one wagon did collapse in the mud, forcing its oldest and weariest passengers to double up with their brothers on the other two wagons. The hardier monks walked the rest of the way. It was still raining when they arrived in Bardstown. They set out in the dark to find St. Joseph's College, a Jesuit-run school where they had been promised a place to sleep.

Here, in Fr. Eutropius' own words, is a description of what happened next:

We arrived at eleven o'clock. The streets were so full of water and mud that we were knee-deep therein. We went directly to St. Joseph's College. Our guides, weary and hungry, left us at its walls and went to a hotel. Our difficulty was to find the entrance, for one could not see a yard ahead.

With two other monks, Dom Eutropius walked around the building looking for some way inside.

We kept on seeking and groping until we succeeded in finding the door. We knocked again and again, but no answer. Not knowing what to do, we called aloud together the word "Trappist." In this we were successful. As soon as the good fathers heard that word they opened the windows.

The Jesuits fed the exhausted monks, who had not stopped to eat along the way but only snacked on cheese, bread and fruit in their wagons. The priests had no empty beds available so the monks bedded down for the night on the floor of the school, wrapped only in light coverlets. The next morning, the feast of St. Thomas the Apostle, the community headed out again in their wagons, knowing that soon they would be home.

Imagine what it must have been like for them that morning of Dec. 21, 1848. The road was most likely quiet, as were the monks, with only the rhythmic creaking of the wagon wheels and the occasional cry of a wild animal breaking the silence. Who can say what emotions stirred in the French Trappists as they entered the valley that encompasses Gethsemani. Gratitude, absolutely. Trepidation, probably. Delight. Homesickness. Curiosity. Relief. Peace. Wherever they looked, they would have seen blue hills in the distance climbing toward a gray December sky.

This protected place, in the middle of nowhere, was Cistercian to its core: desert and paradise inhabiting the same space. Did Fr. Paulinus, the scout who purchased the property the previous year, know a certain satisfaction at the sight of land that matched his memory of it? Did the monks think of their brothers a world away at Melleray? Not two months of prayer and planning at sea nor all the enthusiastic accounts by Frs. Paulinus and Paul could have prepared them for this moment. All we know is that they moved into the buildings the Sisters of Loretto had sold them and celebrated Christmas four days later.

And then, as their neighbors would have put it, all hell broke loose.

ABOVE: *The official proclamation of Fr. Eutropius as prior.*
OPPOSITE: *A rabbet plane used in carpentry by monks.*

62

SURVIVING KENTUCKY:
GETHSEMANI BECOMES an ABBEY

FIRST CAME THE FREEZE: A SUDDEN PLUNGE IN temperature the very first night Fr. Eutropius and his monks spent at Gethsemani. Then there was the matter of their baggage: it seems the bulk of it, including their ovens and cookware, was locked away for two months in a Louisville storehouse. Within a week, the abbot fell seriously ill, laid low by a bout of pneumonia. His recovery came slowly and only after Fr. Paulinus had given him last rites; his health remained a concern to the community for some time.

But that was not all; not nearly. When summer came around, the Ohio Valley heat waves were merciless on the Trappists who, like their brothers in more moderate climates, worked the fields in woolen robes. They tried to fend off the blistering rays of the Kentucky summer sun by pulling their hoods up over their shaved heads, but the sweat-drenched cloth around their faces made them even more uncomfortable. Hearing of their plight, the General Chapter of 1849 granted the community some relief by permitting lighter clothes and straw hats in summer, as they had done for a monastery in North Africa.

Despite the constant challenges to the community's physical stamina, Fr. Paulinus wanted to put his men to work building a monastery. They had already torn down the dilapidated cabins on the property and built an addition to the chapel. Now, while Fr. Eutropius was recovering his strength, Fr. Paulinus ordered the first batch of bricks for the construction project. According to the annals of that period, it took 3,189,240 bricks to complete the monastery – at a cost of $1.50 to $3.50 per thousand, depending on quality. The price tag on the bricks alone would have totaled somewhere between $4,800 and $11,000, a hefty expenditure in those days.

Where did the money come from for this huge project?

As soon as Fr. Eutropius was back on his feet, he began a marathon fund-raising tour of Europe. As he made his rounds during the summer of 1849, seeking donations from patrons big and small, he kept track of the pledges he secured in small leather-bound notebooks. He left no stone unturned on the continent, and in his own words, "roamed quite a lot." In a letter to Dom Maxime, he described how he was getting his message across:

I have explained it in the churches and cathedrals, sometimes to audiences of more than 6,000 people. The newspapers have spoken about it, always very favorably, so that, despite the misfortunes of the times, I have found some assistance to such an extent that now with what has been

MELLERAY'S RESURGENCE

1817: Lulworth monks return to France to reopen Melleray.

1827: Melleray becomes most prosperous of French abbeys.

1831: Monks of Melleray are routed when abbey is occupied by 600 soldiers.

1832: Melleray founds Mount Melleray in Waterford, Ireland.

1837: Monks return to Melleray.

1839: Melleray thrives once more.

1847: Melleray considers foundation in Martinique; Melleray's prior, Father Paulinus, buys Nelson County farm called Gethsemani from Sisters of Loretto.

THE ABBACY OF DOM EUTROPIUS

1848: Melleray monks, led by Fr. Eutropius Proust, leave France October 26.

1849: First two Trappists take vows of stability to Gethsemani; Fr. Eutropius returns to France to raise money; New Melleray in Iowa is founded by Mount Melleray of Ireland.

1850: Trappists of Bellefontaine take over French Benedictine Abbey of Fontgombault and run a penitentiary to make ends meet; Pope Pius IX agrees to make Gethsemani an abbey; Bishop Flaget dies.

1851: Gethsemani becomes "Proto-Abbey of the New World;" Fr. Eutropius elected abbot.

1852: Architect William Keely hired to design three-story monastery; Keely also designed the Cathedral of the Assumption in Louisville, which had recently opened.

1854: U.S. Catholics under attack by anti-immigration Know-Nothing Party.

1859: Dom Eutropius resigns due to poor health and later returns to Melleray.

1874: Dom Eutropius dies at Abbey of Tre Fontane.

promised me at Melleray, my total amount cannot be far from forty thousand francs. I tell you this in secret and confidentially for, if it were known, I would be thought rich and would obtain nothing. However, what is 40,000 francs for building a monastery and starting from nothing? Especially I would not like the Propagation of Faith to have knowledge of this for I am making some advances toward these gentlemen of the Council of Lyon to obtain new aid. I have seen them all, each one in private. I have spoken to them about our situation, about the impressions we have made in that country and about our hopes for the future . . . I have done all I believe that depends on me. Now what the result of my advances will be, I will know only in six weeks to two months.

Let there be no mistake: Fr. Eutropius was a meticulously organized man who knew how to get things done. In the same letter, he reports on current events at Gethsemani, repeating what Fr. Paulinus has been telling him in letters. The "wretched huts" the monks first lived in are now torn down, replaced with large temporary sheds to serve as dormitories until the monastery can be built. Fr. Eutropius also matter-of-factly updates Dom Maxime on the health of his monks and the unexpected hazards of community life:

Brother Paphnutius died shortly after his arrival. Brother Vital was very sick but is now cured. Brother Gervais nearly killed himself by falling 19 feet from the barn. He owes his life, after the assistance of heaven, to a foot of mud which happened to be on the ground where he fell.

Fr. Eutropius also makes it clear that Gethsemani is making a name for itself quickly in the states.

The Archbishop of St. Louis is constantly soliciting a foundation from us. Two other bishops would also like to have us. A landowner in New York wrote me since I was on this trip to offer as much land as I would like and funds to build, if I would send religious without delay to his estates. However advantageous all his offers may be, still I do not think it would be prudent to accept them without having a house at Gethsemani – for before creating, one must exist.

ABOVE: *A hand-written Gethsemani ledger noting expenditures for building the monastery.* RIGHT: *Notebooks kept by Dom Eutropius, Fr. Paulinus and other monks, recording contributions to defray construction costs.*

$400 Twelve months after date I promis to pay Ally Fagan one hundred Dollar for the hir of negro man name Able and to clothe well treat humanly pay doctors Bills if eny But if Able should be sik over fifteen days The said Ally Fagan is to lose the time The value recive This 1 day of January 1853

F. Maria Eutropius
Gethsemani

ABOVE: *A note signed by Dom Eutropius, promising to pay $100 to a neighbor for the hire of a slave laborer.* LEFT: *A pectoral cross worn by Dom Eutropius.*

As for the new recruits to Cistercian life, Fr. Eutropius is frank in his assessment: "A great enough number of postulants come," he writes, "but the trial is too demanding; few persevere." Records show that Melleray was generously sending reinforcements from its community during the first few years.

In 1851, the General Chapter granted Gethsemani the status of "Proto-Abbey of the New World," giving it the right to elect an abbot. In May, Dom Eutropius was elected abbot and in October he was blessed at a ceremony at the old St. Joseph's Cathedral in Bardstown.

By October 1852, Dom Eutropius felt confident enough in the outcome of all his fund-raising to hire architect William Keely to design a three-story monastery modeled on the motherhouse at Melleray.

Keely was the designer of the Cathedral of the Assumption, which had recently opened in Louisville. On March 25, 1853, the feast of the Annunciation, the cornerstone of the Abbey of Gethsemani was laid.

WHEN CONSTRUCTION BEGAN, GETHSEMANI'S NEIGHbors were prominent among the work force. They cut down trees for timber and laid bricks side by side with the monks. More than a few black slaves also worked on the monastery in those pre-Civil War days. In one case, a

66

LEFT: *A receipt for building materials, one of many early documents preserved in the abbey's archives.* BELOW: *A Gethsemani letter dated July 1850, acknowledging receipt of rice from a neighbor, and a sliding bevel square used by monks.*

struction of the monastery, Gethsemani would provide local families with something in short supply at that time – free schools for their sons and daughters.

Though local labor was necessary for such a massive project, the deal ended up costing Gethsemani more than Dom Eutropius bargained for. Over time, maintaining and staffing schools demanded a level of activity and involvement with the outside world that proved incompatible with the contemplative life the monks had vowed to lead.

Gethsemani would ultimately surrender its misbegotten role as educator of young people, but before that could be accomplished the community would have to endure public scandal, the forced resignation of an abbot and a devastating fire.

OPPOSITE: *A rare photograph of Dom Eutropius in his later years.* ABOVE: *His gravestone at Tre Fontane.* RIGHT: *His letter of resignation.*

local planter loaned his slaves to the community as his contribution to the project. In another, the monastery rented a neighbor's slave. The fee went to the slave-owner, of course – not to the slave who did the work.

Gethsemani's neighbors pitched in not only out of goodwill, but also in exchange for a valuable promise made by Dom Eutropius. When the abbot took his fund-raising speech to the local citizenry, he tried a tactic different from any he had used in Europe or, for that matter, elsewhere in America. To his neighbors, he offered a special deal: in return for help with the con-

Dom Eutropius would be long gone by the time this came to pass. He resigned in 1859. In 1860, his declining health prompted him to return to Melleray. The departure of Gethsemani's first abbot saddened the community, which now numbered 65 men. Dom Eutropius would not be there to oversee the completion of the abbey church in 1864, although his health did improve after his return to France. Soon he was serving as abbot again – this time at the Abbey of Tre Fontane, outside Rome, where he died in 1874.

DOM BENEDICT BERGER:
AN EMBATTLED ABBEY FIGHTS for its LIFE
1860-1889

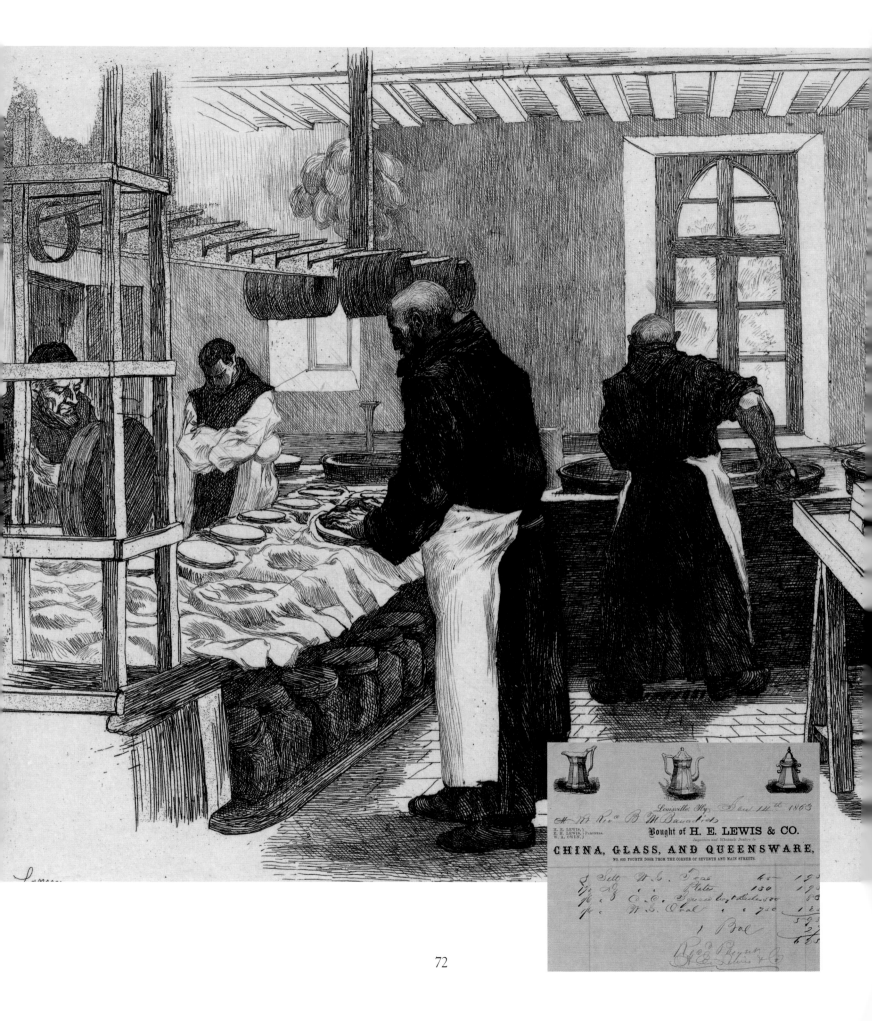

LEFT: *A 19th-century etching of Trappist life and an early receipt for kitchen supplies, including dishes.*
ABOVE: *Lock and key to the vault of the original monastery at Gethsemani.*

GETHSEMANI'S SECOND ABBOT, DOM BENEDICT Berger, was among the original 44 founders from Melleray. Born in 1820, he grew up in the Loire Valley of France, where his father was a small-town merchant who served in Napoleon's army. At the age of 28, Benedict entered Melleray and was a novice there a few months when he joined the colony headed for the New World. He was ordained a priest two years after his arrival at Gethsemani.

Dom Eutropius must have sensed Father Benedict's potential leadership qualities: he made sure the young choir monk learned to speak English fluently and assigned him to key jobs. When the proto-abbot resigned in 1859, he had Benedict in mind as heir apparent.

Yet, from the start, there were signs Dom Benedict was in for a bumpy ride. As events would have it, he was officially installed as abbot on April 19, 1861 – exactly one week after the start of the Civil War.

Some histories maintain that Dom Benedict was the community's choice for abbot because of his highly disciplined personality and scrupulous adherence to the rigorous reforms of La Trappe. Certainly, as abbot, Dom Benedict zealously enforced those austere practices. In *The Waters of Siloe,* Merton suggests his election was a sign of the community's desire to return to a more contemplative way of life after so many years of upheaval and activity as a new foundation. Perhaps they saw an uncompromising monk like Dom Benedict as capable of re-establishing the balance that had been lost.

Yet, Dom Benedict's years in the abbot's office turned out to be decades scarred by conflict – religious, political and personal. The Civil War ravaged Kentucky for four long years, dividing families whose allegiances were mixed and complicating relationships at all levels. After the war, Gethsemani found itself engulfed in controversies with its neighbors as Dom Benedict struggled

to preserve the abbey's monastic identity while still ful-filling its responsibilities to the growing Catholic population. The times demanded a fiercely determined leader of unbending principles, and Dom Benedict by all accounts lived up to this requirement.

BUT THERE WAS ALSO AN AMIABLE AND GREGARIOUS side to Dom Benedict, and it is nowhere better illus-trated than in an 1878 historical narrative that has only recently come to light.

A History of the People Called Monks was written by a contemporary of Dom Benedict, lawyer William B. Allen of Greensburg, Kentucky. Today the manuscript belongs to one of the author's descendants, Ron Pen, associate professor of music at the University of Ken-tucky and director of the John Jacob Niles Center for American Music. Pen donated a transcript of that narra-

tive to the abbey archives.

Allen, a Masonic officer, held several public offices, including Green County Attorney, and was an experi-enced interpreter of Kentucky lore. His *History of Kentucky* was published in 1872. He apparently came to know Dom Benedict quite well over the course of many visits to the abbey. In the preface to his history of the monks, Allen says the abbot approved of his project and authenticated the details of his narrative.

In the process of describing Trappist life at Gethse-mani, Allen paints an intriguing portrait of Dom Benedict. Prior to becoming abbot, Benedict was known to his neighbors as "the business man of the institution," according to Allen. To his monks, he may have seemed a self-effacing spiritual leader, but to outsiders he was a straight-shooting negotiator unafraid to speak his mind or hammer out a deal. Allen describes him this way:

Though a green foreigner, as I heard him call himself, and unable to master American shrewdness, he had the reputation in the neighborhood of being one of the sharpest of traders, always speaking his mind freely, plainly and with determination of purpose.

During the Civil War, soldiers from both sides of the conflict paid visits to the abbey. "Some wanted something to eat, some wanted spirits, others wanted to buy horses," writes Allen. A deeply spiritual man caught in the middle of a profoundly political dispute, the abbot responded to his visitors with all the monastic prudence and Cistercian hospitality he could muster.

During the War of Rebellion, it was Father Benedict's good fortune to be respected by all men in authority, whether officers or others; and it may be said in truth that no man of any pursuits enjoyed a greater popularity; for he was kind, accommodating, charitable and generous. No man ever turned from his door without a morsel for his comfort, whatever might be his necessities, nor whether he belonged to the Federal or Confederate army.

OPPOSITE: *A visit by Kentucky Governor Proctor Knott.* ABOVE LEFT: *Dom Benedict Berger, wearing white, attending the Baltimore Plenary Council.*
ABOVE RIGHT: *Gethsemani's annals, relating a Civil War incident.* LEFT: *A railroad stock certificate.*
BELOW: *A receipt from a Civil War-era Louisville business establishment .*

Monastery of Gethsemane, Ky.

ABOVE: *The Abbey church.* RIGHT: *The preau.* OPPOSITE: *The refectory.*

Monastery of Gethsemane, Ky

ALLEN RELATES A POPULAR STORY THAT APPEARED IN newspapers at the time. It is a wry account of a dramatic meeting between Dom Benedict, a Union sympathizer, and General John H. Morgan, the marauding Confederate officer whose volunteer cavalrymen – known as Morgan's Raiders – caused staggering losses among Union troops.

Apocryphal or not, the story confirms the public view of Dom Benedict as a shrewd operator. It opens with Morgan telling the abbot he wants to buy the abbey's finest horses for his troops. Dom Benedict calmly informs the Rebel officer that he has arrived too late: the best horses have already been sold. When Morgan asks how this could be, the two begin to dance, ever so politely, around a very ticklish issue – the abbot's political allegiance.

"Why," says [the abbot], "hearing you were in the country, and in the meantime having opportunity, I sold them to the Federal or Union army. But I have reserved eleven mares and a number of colts under three years old, which you can get if they will suit you."

"Well let's see them," says Morgan.

So the abbot took him to the barn and showed them to him.

"Why," says Morgan, "your mares are all with foal, and your colts too young for our service, and I would not have as a gracious gift any of them. They do not suit me at all, sir."

Morgan then rounded up his soldiers and promptly took his leave – without laying a hand on the abbot or threatening the monastery in any way. Some time later, the general was defeated in Kentucky and subsequently was killed by Union troops in Tennessee.

On the Union side, Dom Benedict had made an ally of a certain Colonel Pope. According to Allen, Pope ordered his soldiers to respect the monks and provided the abbot and his men with passes to guarantee their

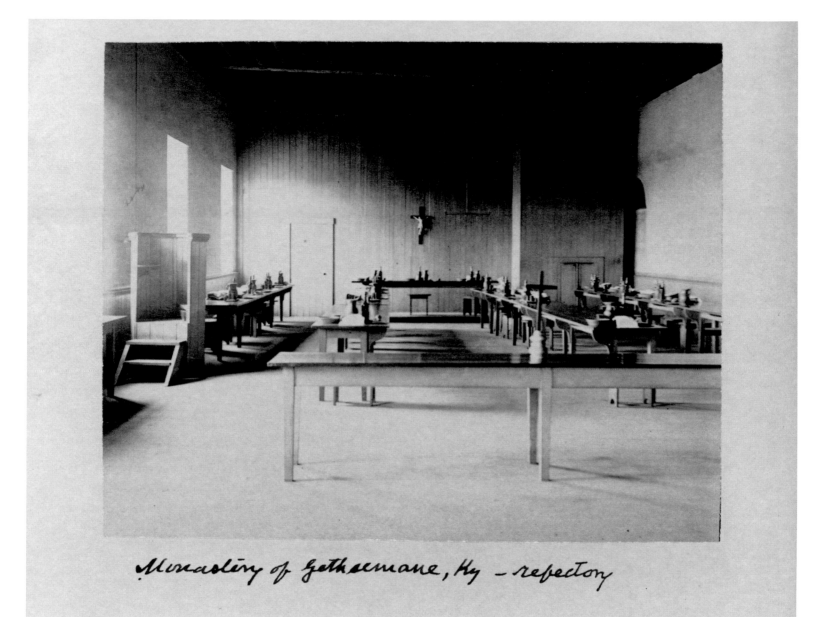

Monastery of Gethsemane, Ky — refectory

THE ABBACY OF DOM BENEDICT

1860: Dom Benedict Berger is named superior in January and elected abbot in December; Abraham Lincoln is elected president.

1861: Civil War begins.

1862: Slavery is abolished in U.S.

1864: Secular church of Gethsemani is dedicated.

1865: Dom Benedict buys Frank Smith's property for Mount Olivet school; Civil War ends; Lincoln is assassinated.

1866: Monastery is dedicated on November 15; American Reform Judaism movement begins.

1870: General Chapter calls for Gethsemani to renounce ties to Mount Olivet; Vatican Council votes that Pope is infallible.

1873: Mount Olivet closes; Jesse James gang robs its first passenger train.

1875: Aristides wins first Kentucky Derby.

1876: Battle of Little Big Horn; telephone is introduced.

1878: Baron Hodiamont De Neau returns.

1881: Pasteur develops vaccine against anthrax; President James Garfield is assassinated.

1889: Dom Benedict resigns.

safety as they went about their business in the neighbor-hood. The following story demonstrates a surprising level of trust and respect between the two.

One night during the war, some officers and soldiers, in their scouts over the knobs at 11 o'clock at night, called at the Abbey and demanded whiskey, which they said they wanted very badly. The abbot gave it to them, remarking to them in the meantime, with his usual freedom, that he would like not to be interrupted anymore in the night time.

"Come," said he, "in the daylight. . . ."

Colonel Pope, being informed of the conduct of his sol-diers . . . by some gentlemen of the town of New Haven where he was then stationed, immediately mounting his horse, he rode full speed to the abbey and in the most humble

Lourdes Grotto, at Gethsemani Abbey.

TOP: *Dom Benedict (first row, extreme left) at the dedication of the abbey church.* ABOVE: *Lourdes Grotto at Gethsemani's secular church.*

manner apologized to the abbot for the conduct of his soldiers, begging his pardon with his hat in hand, and assuring him that such conduct should never happen again toward the monks whilst he had any power to control.

The Colonel was true to his word, Allen concludes. Gethsemani suffered no further breaches of monastic sleep for the duration of the War.

On November 15, 1866, with the War behind it, the community solemnly consecrated its abbatial church. Bishop Martin John Spalding, a lifelong friend of the Trappists, returned from Baltimore to deliver the homily, and a crowd of priests and religious leaders participated in the celebration. Two years earlier, on May 1, 1864, the "secular church" – the public portion of Gethsemani's Gothic-Revival basilica – had been dedicated as a place of worship for Catholics in the neighborhood. Melleray sent a French priest, Father Jerome Moyen, to serve as pastor of the abbey congregation.

About the same time, at Bishop Spalding's request, Gethsemani took charge of a neighboring congregation, St. Vincent's, which had been expanded to include parts of other local parishes. Fr. Jerome and later another priest, Nicholas Ryan, were to serve as pastors, under Gethsemani's supervision.

In 1866, Dom Benedict also established a women's religious group, known as the Third Order of St. Francis, and assigned its sisters to teach at Gethsemani's new Mount Olivet Female Primary School.

Despite these growing relationships between the abbey and the neighborhood (and in some cases, because of them), Gethsemani's reputation remained, in Merton's words, "not altogether a pleasant one to most minds." In *The Waters of Siloe* he attributes this hostile image, in part, to Dom Benedict's "ruthless" adherence to The Rule.

Allen confirms that the public is suspicious (if not downright fearful) of what goes on behind cloister walls. But he also dismisses those fears as misconceived. In the end, his rebuttal of the most common "charges" against the Trappists reveals as much about the public's lack of familiarity with monasticism in general, as it does about their views of Gethsemani in particular. Allen recites a litany of rumor and gossip.

It is charged of the monks that they bind themselves in a moment of mistaken fervor, and that they are an unhappy race of beings. These charges [the monks] pronounce utterly false....

It is charged against the monks that they seek after the fortunes of the postulants. All they demand of those who present themselves for reception into their congregation is, as they say, virtue and devotion.

On the other hand, Allen pulls no punches when describing the stern discipline that Gethsemani's monks experienced under Dom Benedict. Reading his blunt descriptions of Trappist life, one has to wonder whether he allayed the public's fears, or fanned them. A typical passage follows:

During two-thirds of the year, they eat but once in 24 hours. This meal consists of soup seasoned with salt and water in herbs. . . . Two planks, a straw mattress covered with a coarse sheet, a woolen blanket and a pillow stuffed with straw is all that is required for the repose of the monks. . . .

When one has been guilty of a grievous fault he has to perform penance for it. He begins by taking the discipline in the chapter, in other words, he whips himself over the naked shoulders. The whip is made of a cord, which has five divisions, each with five knots in it. When the time of his penance has expired, he prostrates himself on the knuckles before the superiors and religious, and these standing, he listens to the admonitions of the superior. Penances of light faults are such as taking his meal after the community in a different place . . . prostrations at the door of the refectory . . . eating on the floor a piece of bread only with a jug of water . . . [or] sometimes he performs his penance by kissing the feet of the religious beginning with the abbot.

DOM BENEDICT MAY HAVE INTENSIFIED THE SPIRITual life of his monks, but his austere rule did little to bolster the size of the community. In its first 30 years, only eight American-born men entered Gethsemani, and not one of them stayed. The "Proto-Abbey of the New World" was under constant threat of being closed. By 1878, the community numbered only 43 men, fewer than the original band of founders.

Fearful that the abbey might become too small in the future to support itself, Dom Benedict began leasing acreage to local farmers who, in exchange for working the land, shared in its profit. In 1884, Gethsemani's grain

mill burned to the ground. That meant the monastery had to come up with even more money and manpower.

Though no one could have known it at the time, the tide began to turn in 1885. That year, John Green Hanning, a Texas cowboy who had grown up on a Kentucky tobacco farm, entered Gethsemani as a lay brother. He

would later be honored as the first U.S.-born citizen to live out his life as a professed member of the community. He would become the bridge between Gethsemani's French past and its all-American future.

At that time, Gethsemani was running a large, busy farm. In his narrative, Allen writes that the abbey employed the best scientific techniques and used the most up-to-date equipment. He compares the industrious efficiency of its work crews to that of a "swarm of bees" – minus the droning.

You hear the din and noise of agricultural and mechanical industry, without hearing a word spoken among them, for they speak only to their superiors and officers.

The monks raised livestock, and their storehouses were well-stocked with barrels of homemade cider, wine and apple brandy, the fruits of their orchards. On

one visit to Gethsemani, Allen sampled a three-year-old cider produced by the monks and found it "superior to the best wine I ever drank."

Allen praises the monks as "more saving of manure than any farmers I have ever known," and links their liberal use of homegrown fertilizer to the farm's high productivity. He estimates Gethsemani's livestock population at roughly 50 head of cattle, 40 head of horses, over a hundred hogs and "a good many sheep." Wool from the sheep was sold for income, but most other farm products, including cheese, butter and milk, were consumed inside the monastery.

By the end of Dom Benedict's regime, the community had dwindled to 34 men. The strain of supervising schools, parishes and a sisterhood was taking its toll. In the end, none of these outside enterprises would endure, and frankly few at the abbey would mourn their passing.

In 1889, confined to a wheelchair, his health failing fast, Dom Benedict resigned as abbot. He retired to the infirmary, where he would die the following August at the age of 71. Fr. Paulinus, the onetime scout and long-time prior, had a decade earlier returned to Melleray to die; so it was the new prior, Father Edward Chaix-Bourbon, who was elected to succeed Dom Benedict.

Hopes were high for the new abbot who seemed destined to lead Gethsemani into the 20th century. Too high, as it turned out. Dom Edward would be gone before the century turned. And Gethsemani, plagued by crisis and criticism, would be forced to face the awesome task of rebuilding itself.

THE STORY of MOUNT OLIVET

Gethsemani School.

IN JUNE OF 1865, FRANK SMITH OF NELSON COUNTY sold a plot of land with two buildings on it to the Abbey of Gethsemani. According to the deed, the four corners of the Smith property, located near Pottinger's Creek, were marked respectively by a plank fence and three easily identifiable landmarks: an elm, a black oak and a poplar stump.

But Dom Benedict didn't see the land in terms of trees or boundaries. He saw it simply as an answer to a prayer. He needed a place to build a school to serve the female children of the neighborhood. More than a decade earlier, his predecessor, Dom Eutropius, had vowed to educate all the children who lived in the area in exchange for their families' support while Gethsemani was building its monastery. The neighbors had responded generously, and Dom Eutropius had built a boys school as his part of the bargain. Now it was time for Dom Benedict to do the same for the girls.

Dom Eutropius had already set up a small brick schoolhouse on a spot known as Calvary Hill and hired teachers to instruct local girls. But when Dom Benedict took office, he felt it was necessary to get permission from his Trappist superiors to maintain the school, which he feared violated the contemplative mission of the order. He was given the go-ahead, however – with the understanding that he was to groom an order of sis-

ters to take over the school's operation. An agreement regarding the school was worked out between Bishop Spalding of Baltimore and the Trappist Abbot Bruno of Ireland.

Now, in 1865, Dom Benedict saw the Smith property as the perfect setting for an expanded girls school. He and his monks set out to repair the existing buildings for use as temporary quarters for a convent and school. On May first of the following year, the Mount Olivet Female Primary School was officially blessed and opened for business. Plans were approved for a new schoolhouse on the property.

In the meantime, Dom Benedict had established a women's religious association, The Third Order of St. Francis, whose members agreed to run the school. According to abbey records from that era, the day school was free to all students "without distinction of creed." Girls from the neighborhood were given priority in admissions but those from outlying areas were welcome.

The boarding school was free to poor girls, 12 and older. Those who could afford tuition paid $48 a six-month session; laundry and bedding were $12 extra. All the girls were taught spelling, reading, writing, arithmetic, grammar, art, music, geography and "the common household works suited to females."

The new school, built with much help from the

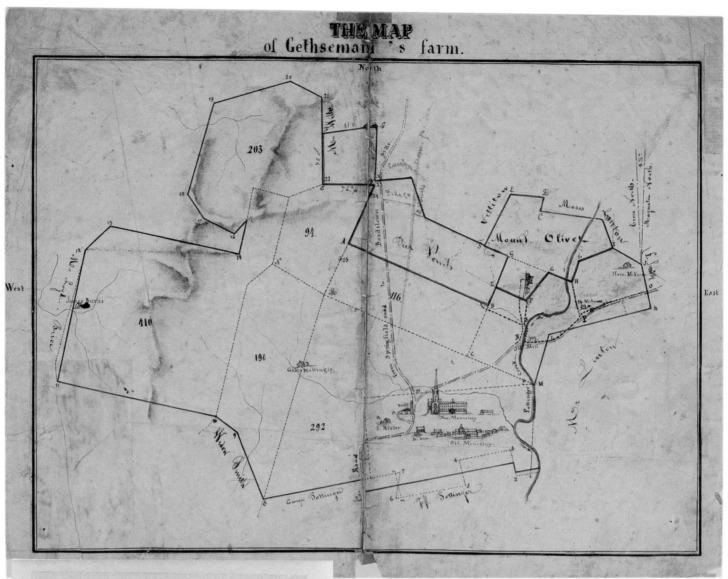

THE MAP
of Gethsemani's farm.

Gethsemane Monastery Ky.

TOP: *Earliest map of Gethsemani property.* ABOVE: *Pieta shrine on Calvary Hill, southwest of the monastery and west of the boys' school.* OPPOSITE: *Boys seated in front of a building on the Mount Olivet campus.*

brothers at Gethsemani, was a three-story frame structure with a wood-burning hot-air furnace, a rarity in those days, and a wrap-around porch that resembled the prow of a steamship.

THE FIRST MEMBER OF THE THIRD ORDER WAS Caroline Warren, a widow whose husband died in the Civil War Battle of Perryville in 1862. Mrs. Warren – who became known as Sister Elizabeth – was in her mid-30s in 1863, when she confided to Dom Benedict that she was interested in becoming a nun.

At that time, according to the Gethsemani annals, the abbot asked her to take over as supervisor of the girls school. The following year, she became the first to take the habit of the Third Order community, which was

ABOVE: *The Congregation of the Sisters of St. Francis of the Immaculate Conception of Clinton, Iowa. One of the original three founders of Mount Olivet, Sister M. Francis Walker, is second from left in the front row.* OPPOSITE: *Gethsemani students visiting Mount Olivet.*

commonly known as the Franciscan Tertiaries. Soon two other local women on the school staff joined her. Bishop Lavialle approved their plans for taking over the school and, in keeping with Dom Benedict's dream, changed their name to the Sisters of the Order of La Trappe of Mount Olivet.

Since Mount Olivet had no novitiate, a group of novices were sent to the Franciscan convent in Oldenburg, Indiana, to be trained. Sr. Elizabeth, a woman with deep roots in the neighborhood, served as temporary superior, and two sisters stayed with her to run the school in the novices' absence.

Dom Eutropius, who had been living in France for several years then, happened to visit Gethsemani the summer the school opened. He was delighted to see his promise fulfilled and to hear that the Third Order sisters were interested in eventually becoming Trappistine

nuns. Dom Eutropius congratulated Dom Benedict and left Kentucky feeling that his proto-abbey was in good order.

In truth, Dom Eutropius had been witness to the calm before the storm.

The clouds broke in the summer of 1869, following an election at Mount Olivet. Sister Paula, who had received her training at the Oldenburg novitiate, was elected permanent superior, a situation that upset Sr. Elizabeth. Wounded by the fact that her sisters had not chosen her to continue to lead them, she reluctantly accepted her new assignment as head of the branch school on Calvary Hill.

From the start, however, Sr. Elizabeth shared her grievances with anyone who would listen, including the French priest, Fr. Jerome Moyen, who served as spiritual director to the sisters. The argument created a split within the families of Mount Olivet students, and dis-

sension broke out among neighbors. Even Fr. Jerome took sides in the dispute, supporting Sr. Elizabeth over Sr. Paula, the former Mary Jane Beaven of Union County, Kentucky.

The controversy created division within the ranks of the Kentucky clergy as well, pitting Dom Benedict against Bishop Lavialle's successor, Bishop William McCloskey. For his part, Fr. Jerome was promptly called home to France by his superiors.

Dom Benedict upheld the election and, like some of the sisters, blamed Sr. Elizabeth's defiant attitude on her lack of formal novitiate training. It was clear to Dom Benedict that no one had taught her the meaning of obedience in religious life. Sr. Elizabeth later left the order, sued the abbey for back pay and settled out of court for the sum of $2,500, according to one version of the story. A neighbor and longtime patron of Gethsemani, Ben

Mattingly, paid off the abbey's debt to Sr. Elizabeth, who then moved to Nashville. Mattingly had once before settled a debt on the sisters' land to satisfy Bishop McCloskey, who worried that the women would not be able to pay it and he would be held liable.

Although the abbot did his best to put the matter to rest, feelings had been hurt, and the healing took time. Meanwhile Gethsemani was trying to run two parishes (one at the abbey and one at nearby St. Vincent's) in addition to operating two schools. The monks were feeling the strain of so much outside activity.

The following March, yet another problem arose. Some years earlier, Father Nicholas Ryan, a priest from Ireland, had contracted with Gethsemani to live at the monastery until he died, serving as a pastor in exchange for having his material needs met by the abbey. Gethsemani had assisted him in his training for the priesthood in Baltimore and gave him room and board at the abbey.

But now Fr. Ryan was asking to leave the monastery and live on his own. He would continue to perform his work for the abbey, but now he wished to be paid. Dom Benedict allowed him to wiggle out of his contract, but then Fr. Ryan began neglecting the sisters, who in turn complained to Dom Benedict. Following that unpleasant controversy, Fr. Ryan moved out of the area, leaving Gethsemani with no priests at all to help run its parishes and schools. Dom Benedict was forced to assign his own choir monks to do the work. Ultimately, the parishes were surrendered to the diocese.

The General Chapter had never liked the idea of Gethsemani taking on so many outside responsibilities but had felt compelled to approve the schools and parishes in light of Fr. Eutropius' promise. Now, however, upkeep of the schools and property, which the abbey had expanded with the purchase of an adjoining farm, were not only a constant drain on the contemplative life, but they were a source of increasing turmoil within the local diocese.

Relations with Bishop McCloskey, never comfortable, were severely strained by the conflict over Mount Olivet. According to several contemporary accounts, the bishop believed the nuns were needed more in the diocese's outlying parishes. He worked behind the scenes to remove the sisters from Gethsemani's jurisdiction and began urging Sister Paula to move to another part of Kentucky.

Push came to shove in 1870. That year, despite the support of Bishop Spalding and other members of the Catholic hierarchy, the Trappist General Chapter sent Dom Benedict what seemed like an all-too-clear message: detach from Mount Olivet. Dom Bruno of Ireland arrived at Gethsemani for a visitation, prepared to cut the ties between the school and the abbey. However, after meeting with the nuns and hearing their desire to stay at Mount Olivet, Dom Bruno worked out a last-minute compromise between abbey and diocese.

Dom Bruno's visit is recorded in the abbey annals this way: "The girls sang for him. He seemed delighted with the quiet of the place. He said before long we would have a large convent, nearly as large as the monastery."

The peace was short-lived, however. Controversies continued to grow up around the school to the point that, in 1873, Gethsemani gave in to the mounting pressures. Mount Olivet was closed, the nuns moved to Shelbyville, and the property and sisterhood that Dom Benedict had once considered an answer to his prayer seemed lost. The sisters briefly attempted to revive the school a few years later, but the effort failed and once again the school was empty.

That last good-bye marked a turning point for the community of women who had once dreamed of becoming Trappistines. In 1890, at the invitation of the bishop of Dubuque, the Mount Olivet sisters left Kentucky to make a foundation, known as The Congregation of Sisters of St. Francis of the Immaculate Conception in Clinton, Iowa. By the time they left, Dom Benedict – their tireless supporter – was dead, and the new abbot, Edward Chaix-Bourbon, was glad to see the school close and the nuns gone.

For a time after the nuns' departure, Mount Olivet was home to a female mystic who befriended Dom Edward. Then it briefly housed a boys school. Under Dom Edmond Obrecht, it was for two years a makeshift monastery for a community of exiled French monks. Later, the Boone family, neighbors of the abbey, bought the building and lived in it, then sold it back to the abbey.

Until recently, it stood as a monument to the would-be Trappistine community and the Mount Olivet school for girls. In the summer of 1995, however, a fire destroyed the old building where the sisters founded their order, taking with it one of the last traces of a most intriguing chapter of Gethsemani's story.

A GHOST from GETHSEMANI'S PAST:
BARON HODIAMANT DE NEAU

PERHAPS NAME WAS DESTINY FOR BARON JOHN LAMBERT Emmanuel Amor Constant de Hodiamont de Neau. Who could lead an ordinary life with such an extraordinary name?

Whatever the reasons for his exceptional personal history, Hodiamont is without doubt one of the most vibrant and intriguing Old World characters in Gethsemani's history. Born in 1789, he grew up in a noble family of the old duchy of Limbourg. At the age of 14, with the lukewarm blessing of his parents, he joined the company of Dom Urban Guillet and his band of Trappists on their trek to America in 1803.

For a decade, Hodiamont willingly shared Dom Urban's vagabond way of life, making settlements and then moving on, from Pennsylvania to Kentucky into Missouri and Illinois. But he put his foot down when Urban announced his intentions to leave the frontier entirely and return to New York. Apparently the West agreed with Hodiamont.

At 24, then, he decided to stay put in the Mississippi valley and let the monks leave without him. His instincts had not led him astray. Soon he was pursuing a prosperous career as a merchant in St. Louis. A natural entrepreneur, he gradually built his business into a fortune. He married, raised a family and later in his full, rich life drew on his great wealth and wisdom to get the nation's first streetcar system up and running.

In 1878, however, he left that life behind. Hodiamont returned to Kentucky to reacquaint himself with the Trappist life he had been drawn to as a teenager. By then he was nearly 90, though by all reports he looked much younger. He still had a strong mind, and he knew precisely what he wanted – to live out the rest of his life within the walls of a monastery.

And that's how, one day, he turned up at Gethsemani's door, beseeching Dom Benedict to take him in as a boarder. Delighted to meet one of Urban's legendary colony, Dom Benedict naturally agreed to Hodiamont's request. It was a generous response, based on affection and admiration. In retrospect, it was also a shrewd decision, one that would prove financially beneficial to the community at a time when its budget was thin and its future uncertain.

During his brief stay, Hodiamont used his fortune to reduce Gethsemani's debt, including what was owed on Mount Olivet. When he died, the year after his arrival, the Trappists honored him with burial in their cemetery. His gravestone still stands, its inscription reminding all who read it that the Baron was, indeed, "Gethsemani's true friend and munificent benefactor."

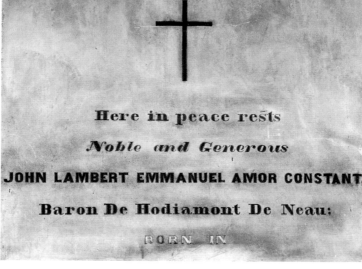

Here in peace rests
Noble and Generous
JOHN LAMBERT EMMANUEL AMOR CONSTANT,
Baron De Hodiamont De Neau;
BORN IN

Dom Edward Chaix-Bourbon:
the Gloom Descends
1890-1895

Fath. Abbot.

Bro. M. Edward

ABOVE: *A view of Gethsemani College on the hillside south of the monastery.*
RIGHT: *An early cheese label.*
OPPOSITE: *The pectoral cross of Dom Edward Chaix-Bourbon.*

90

T RAPPISTS LIKE TO SAY THAT A HOUSE ALWAYS GETS the abbot it needs, even though at the time its monks may not realize it. It is certainly true that for most of Gethsemani's 150 years the right leader has come along at the right time.

But in the case of Dom Edward Chaix-Bourbon, the third abbot of Gethsemani, the hard, cold facts of history do not support this optimistic maxim. Dom Edward, a kindly but weak administrator, was not at all what the abbey needed in 1890 when he succeeded Dom Benedict Berger. An agreeable, good-humored man, he made friends easily but not wisely. If ever there were a time when the abbey needed skillful leadership and heroic vision, this was it. Neither a leader nor a hero, Dom Edward seems – in hindsight – simply the wrong man for the job.

Trappists have another saying about their leaders, however, and this one seems to apply quite accurately to Dom Edward's regime: a house elects each of its abbots as a corrective to the one who came before. For example, an industrious abbot who keeps his monks busy and his monastery active is likely to be succeeded by a man with a well-known love of silence and simplicity. In other words, a Trappist community maintains its spiritual equilibrium over time by electing abbots who differ in significant ways from their predecessors. This self-regulating balancing act often occurs even when the outgoing abbot is well-loved and respected. Change, then, becomes an essential part of the long-term rhythm of community life.

Certainly Dom Edward was a change from Dom Benedict. Where Dom Benedict ruled swiftly and with an iron will, Dom Edward hesitated, vacillated, procrastinated and ultimately postponed any decision he was forced to contemplate. Where Dom Benedict was stern but disciplined, Dom Edward was compassionate but indecisive.

Some historians, including Merton, point to Dom Edward's long-suffering relationship with Dom Benedict as an explanation for his meekness as abbot. Apparently Dom Edward was the frequent victim of his abbot's harsh criticism. Perhaps, when he became abbot, he wanted to prove that a benevolent leader could be as effective as a severe one. Unfortunately, Dom Edward's goodwill got in the way of his good judgment, and this led to Gethsemani's near-demise.

EDWARD CHAIX-BOURBON WAS BORN IN A SMALL town near Grenoble, France. He studied painting and pharmacy as a young man and emigrated to the United States after a brief stint as a broker in France. When Edward entered Gethsemani in 1861, Dom Benedict asked if the "Bourbon" in his name signified some connection to royalty. Edward assured him it did not, which led Benedict to insist he drop the name. The implication was that to falsely associate himself with royalty, however innocently, was an act of vanity. It was only after the community chose him as the third abbot of Gethsemani, nearly three decades later, that "Bourbon" reattached itself to Edward's name. Or so the story goes.

One thing is sure: Dom Edward came into office at a significant moment in Trappist history. In 1892, after much deliberation, the three congregations of the Strict

Chapitre Général DES Abbés Cisterciens.

*tenu à ROME en 1892, pour la réunion des
des trois Observances de la TRAPPE en un seul Ordre.*

OPPOSITE: *The gatehouse bell and early photograph of the monastery.* ABOVE: *Dom Edward, second row, seventh from left, at the General Chapter meeting in Rome in 1892.*

Observance (La Trappe, Westmalle and Septfons) were to become a united order in their own right, no longer dependent on the abbot general of the Common Observance. This would mark the beginning of the international Trappist Order as we know it today.

Perhaps, as he took office, Dom Edward was wondering what role his abbey would play in the new order. Certainly one of his first actions as abbot was a bold one. He elevated the boys' boarding school to the status of a college.

THE ABBACY OF DOM EDWARD

1890: Edward Chaix-Bourbon is elected abbot; Battle of Wounded Knee ends last major resistance to white settlement in America.

1892: Three Strict Observance orders are reunited into one Order of the Cistercians of the Strict Observance (Trappists); Henry Ford road-tests his first motor car.

1895: Gethsemani College scandal breaks; Edward's resignation is rejected; first commercial movie is shown in New York.

1896: Prior Benedict Dupont is named superior.

1898: Father Edmond Obrecht arrives at Gethsemani.

At first blush, the decision seemed wise. Kentucky promptly granted the college authority to confer degrees. Dom Edward was able to borrow the $10,000 needed to enlarge the buildings and equip them with steam heat. Applications for admission began pouring in from all over Kentucky and the states surrounding it.

Dom Edward was so encouraged by these developments that he decided to expand the monastery's educational domain. He used the vacant Mount Olivet property, which had been occupied briefly by a "lady visionary," to house a boarding school for boys who couldn't afford the tuition charged by the college.

There was obviously a need for such schools: the classrooms and dormitories were brimming over in no time. The student body grew to the point that Dom Edward had to reinforce the faculty and staff with his own monks and lay brothers. The community, which was dwindling in size, felt stretched thin by these additional responsibilities.

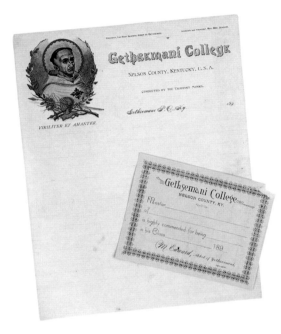

Although Dom Edward sympathized with his men, he saw no alternative but to assign them to the flourishing school. He would prefer having professionals, not contemplatives, in charge; but Dom Edward didn't know where to begin to find them.

Into the midst of Dom Edward's dilemma waltzed Darnley Beaufort – fluent speaker of several languages and dashing pretender to British nobility. Once again, an abbot of Gethsemani thought he saw an answer to a prayer when, in fact, he was looking at a calamity waiting to happen. Beaufort charmed Dom Edward with his big ideas for the college and his dazzling personality. In no time, the abbot hired him to run the boys' boarding school and then promoted him to principal of the college. Beaufort's grand plans captivated the community as well, and for a time it seemed this genial newcomer would help put Gethsemani College on the map.

What he did, instead, was put the abbey in headlines. Screaming, lurid, accusatory headlines. Headlines that splashed across the front pages of Kentucky's newspapers for weeks on end. Gethsemani was suddenly embroiled in the worst sort of scandal a monastery could imagine: its school and its chief administrator stood accused of sexually abusing students.

A gloom descended on the monastery, and it didn't lift for years. Before the skies were to clear, Beaufort would land in jail on charges of fraud, Dom Edward would be forced into early retirement in France, and Gethsemani would face the possibility of losing its Trappist affiliation.

BEAUFORT'S MISBEHAVIOR MAY HAVE SHOCKED READERS of the local newspapers, but the accusations surely came as no surprise to Dom Edward. He had heard his monks' complaints over the years. Beaufort touched students inappropriately, they said. He was too free with physical gestures of affection. They claimed he was not the right person to be running a boys school. Some urged Dom Edward to confront Beaufort and replace him.

But the abbot hesitated, paralyzed by indecision. Rumors spread, and Beaufort kept his job without even so much as a stern warning.

By the fall of 1895, the community was losing its confidence in Dom Edward, and he knew it. He

TOP: *The college band.* ABOVE:
A diploma. RIGHT: *A view of the*
college. OPPOSITE: *The college*
letterhead picturing St. Bernard.

decided the only way out of the mess was to resign. He sailed to France for the General Chapter and, once there, handed over a letter of resignation to the recently elected abbot general of the newly united order. To Dom Edward's shock, the abbot general refused to accept his resignation. Essentially he told him to stop running from the problem and face it squarely.

Dom Edward returned to Gethsemani in October. There he found that the community had learned in his absence that the police were investigating Beaufort. Taking the matter into their own hands, the college directors, five of whom were Trappists, fired Beaufort, adding fraud and embezzlement charges to the list of his offenses.

Some in the community blamed Dom Edward for the crisis and urged him to resign. By this time, he was physically debilitated, plagued by complications from his diabetes and emotionally depleted by the scandal. Two days after his return to Kentucky, on October 23, 1895, he headed back to France to resubmit his resignation. To his dismay, the resignation was again rejected. Even worse, the order decided to ignore the whole matter, leaving the Kentucky community unsure of its future. This time, Dom Edward stayed in France, too sick to leave.

The worst suffering for Gethsemani was yet to come. Left in the cold, unsure of its status as a Trappist house and without an acting superior, the community muddled along. Father Frederic Dunne, the monastery's

ABOVE: *Darnley Beaufort.* OPPOSITE: *Press coverage of the Gethsemani College scandal was mostly supportive of the Trappists in their conflict with Beaufort. This front page of a Louisville newspaper was an exception.*

only American-born choir monk at the time, took charge of the troubled college. Father Benedict Dupont, as prior, was running the monastery. He was well respected as one of those who had long urged Dom Edward to take action against Beaufort; but he was an older man, wise enough to know Gethsemani needed a more vigorous leader.

He and others repeatedly sent letters to Melleray and Rome, begging for advice and direction. None were answered. Months went by, and the community began to fear the worst: it had been abandoned by its motherhouse and order. Finally, in the summer of 1896, two French Trappists paid a visit to Gethsemani to investigate its problems. Their first step was to make it official that Prior Benedict was Gethsemani's superior, but that was hardly encouraging to the community. They needed an abbot, and the visitors did not authorize an election.

Another six months passed with no news. The abbot of Melleray was giving his American daughterhouse the silent treatment. For all practical purposes, Melleray had dismissed its daughterhouse. Dom Francis Strunk, the abbot of Our Lady of Oelenberg in Alsace, had assumed the role of Gethsemani's Father Immediate. Behind the scenes, he and the new abbot general, Dom Sebastian Wyart, were working on a solution. Dom Sebastian knew leadership was what Gethsemani lacked, and he was determined to find just the right man to rebuild the failing house.

THE ABBEY OF GETHSEMANI, KENTUCKY

THE ABBEY OF GETHSEMANI,
NELSON COUNTY, KENTUCKY.

ABOVE AND OPPOSITE: *Two early Gethsemani postcards.*
LEFT: *An engraving from the 1898 Jubilee book.*

In January of 1898, he found him. Father Edmond Obrecht, a Trappist who had held many high offices in the order, was named the new superior of Our Lady of Gethsemani Abbey.

Obrecht arrived in Kentucky on March 25, 1898. Dom Edward's resignation had been accepted and he was by then living at the Trappistine monastery of Our Lady des Gardes near Chenille, France. An election was held, and this time, the community elected a powerful leader to be their abbot: Dom Edmond.

The scandal was finally dying down, though the abbey's reputation was far from what it once had been. From his jail cell, Beaufort was writing pamphlets denouncing the monks and their schools, and rumors still cast a pall on the Trappist way of life.

Dom Edmond had his work cut out for him.

He urged his monks to look to the future with faith and hope. "Providence has sent me, a stranger, into your midst," he told his community, according to the 1949 history, *Burnt Out Incense,* by Gethsemani's Father Raymond Flanagan. Dom Edmond vowed, for his part, to put Gethsemani's problems behind him and to remain "a stranger to all that is dark" in its past.

Depending on how you look at it, that old Trappist saying about houses getting the abbots they need might apply to Dom Edward's election after all. If he had not been a weak leader who put his monks in the gravest danger, an outsider the likes of Edmond Obrecht might never have been sent to straighten things out.

But Dom Edward *did* jeopardize the good name of his monks, and a stranger *was* sent into their midst to give them courage and direction. And that, as the poet said, has made all the difference.

tory of Gethsemani on July 26, 1861,
the habit October 6.
lowing year he
ed his theo-
n he was or-

lious life.
His successor is the Rt. Rev. Edmund
Obrecht, D. D., whose blessing took
place in October, 1898, and, under whose
auspices was solemnly celebrated the
golden jubilee of the abbey.

CATHOLIC REGIS[TER] AND

"VERITAS LIBERABIT VOS!"—THE TRUTH WILL MAK[E]

NEW YORK, SATURDAY, JUNE 17, 1899.

Scene At the Famous Trappist Monastery In Nelson Co.

June 4 1899

CONSECRATION IN THE CHAPEL.

ABBOT EUTROPIUS, O. C. R.,
FOUNDER OF THE ABBEY OF GETHSEMANI.

sway, but we attest that if the gift were
ours to give, we would bestow
Him with all our heart, and
humbly ask Him to vouchsafe to a
it from us, even though it already be
longs to Him.

This is the sense of the act of which
We speak, and such is the true sense of
Our words. And since the Sacred Heart
is recognized as a symbol and clear
image of the infinite charity of Jesus
Christ drawing us to love Him in return
for the appropriateness of offering ourselves to His most august Heart
patent. By doing so we dedicate ourselves and draw closer to Jesus Christ,
for every act of honor, homage and devotion to that Divine Heart is, in the
true and strict sense, directed to the
very person of Jesus Christ.

We stimulate, therefore, and exhort to
the spontaneous fulfillment of the act
all who know and love the Most
Heart, and We earnestly desire
be done by all on the same
the outpouring of thousands
sands of hearts making the same offering may all ascend together to the throne
of God.

[E]DWARD DEAD.

...ration of which
... the aid of all;
be ... carrying on this act, every
one who knows and loves Jesus Christ
will easily experience an increase of
faith and love. Some who, although
knowing Christ, neglect His precepts and
His law, may be enabled to draw from
that Sacred Heart the fire of charity.
Finally, for those who are the most
hopeless, in that they are still involved
in the darkness of superstition, we shall
all unanimously ask heavenly aid in order that Jesus Christ, who already
"holds them potentially subject to Him,"
may at least make them so in very deed,
and not alone "in the next world, when
He will fully achieve His will on all,
destining som... ward and others to
punishmen... n. l. c.), but even
during this... life, by the gift of
... and sanc... on, so that, illumin-
... may duly honor
... eternal happi-
... in heaven.

This consecration will, moreover,
bring hope of more prosperous life to the

ABBOT EDWARD DEAD.

New Haven Echo

Passes Peacefully Away at The
Trappistine Monastery Near
Chenille. France.

March 2 1901

Was Superior of Gethsemani Abbey
at One Time. Brief Sketch
Of His Life.

The sad intelligence of the death
of Right Rev. Father Maria Edward, former Abbot of Gethsemani
Abbey at the Trappistine Monastery of Our Lady des Gardes, near
Chenille, France on February 16,
1901, has been received at the Abbey with the deepest regret, although the news of his demise was
not unexpected, for it was on account of ill health that he had resigned as Abbot of Gethsemani
Abbey and had returned to his native land, France where it was
hoped that the balmy air would
lengthen his days on earth.

Abbot Edward was well known

ter his collegiate course was finished he spent several years in
traveling. He first landed on this
Continent at New Orleans and
from that city he came to Gethsemani where he entered the Monastery on the 26 day of July 1861,
on the following Oct. 6th he took
the habit and made his vows on
November 1st after which he com-
menced his theological studies and
in due time was ordained a priest.
During his life in the Abbey he
served in many positions which
admirably fitted him for the later
responsibilities that fell on his
shoulders.

On Sept. 2, 1889, Abbot Maria
Benedict resigned on account of
ill health; on that day Father Edward was appointed Superior to
serve until the election of an Abbot which occurred on the 3rd of
the following May, when he was
elected third Abbot of Gethsemani

Record

DEAT[H] OF [M]a[r]ia

The Right Rev. M. Edward, O.C.[R.]
Resigned Abbot of the Abbey of
Gethsemane.

Catholics, as also our non-C[atholic]
brethren, of the Diocese of [Louis]-
ville, will be deeply pained t[o learn]
of the death of the gentle and [saintly]
Right Reverend M. Edward, O.C.[R.]
resigned Abbot of the Abbey [of]
Gethsemane, in Nelson County. [He]
died on the 16th of February, 190[1]
at the Monastery of the Trappistin[e]
of Notre Dame des Gardes, Franc[e]
This sad intelligence reaches us
through his successor, the Right Reverend Edmond M. Obrecht, O.C.R.,
present Abbot of Gethsemani, just
as we are going to Press. Time, in
consequence, is not ours to-day to
speak of this dear, departed soul,
who in life, as also in death, was,
and is, one of our attached personal

Go... Fo[r]
are s[o]
wonde[r]
been
tempe[r]
and da[y]
the so[ul]
are sh[own]
God s[o]
selves
their
own li[fe]

Henc[e]
threate[n]
dering
aid in
aid ca[n]
Only B[y]
name
earth
IV. 12)
recour[se]
Truth
astray
road.
ened?
by the
threate[n]
life.
to hea[r]
right r[...]
peace
honor,
scabba[rd]
men's
acknow[l]
obedie[nce]
confess[ed]
in the [...]
II. 11).

Whil[e]
oppress[ed]
a cros[s]
young
and th[...]
that i[s]
before
auspic[es]
... and sh[...]
zling b[...]
our ho[...]
for our [...]

Fina[lly]
anothe[r]
self pe[...]
and im[...]
this ac[t]
of all b[...]
from a[...]
that a [...]
gratitu[de]
greater
now pr[...]

Henc[e]
tha[...]
n that
a prepa[re]
Rev. M[...]
holy [...]
den's t[...]
approve[d]
year... to
piness t[...]
His su[...]
M. Obre[cht]
readers [...]
United [...]

... the cle[rgy]
care as [...]
token o[f]
Given [...]
25th of [...]
year of [...]

Form [...]

O. Sw[...]
human [...]
trate be[fore]
desire t[o]
may liv[e]
hold! w[...]
day spo[...]
to your [...]
have ne[ver]
your co[...]
both the [...]
have me[...]
holy He[...]
alone o[r]
separate[d]
of those [...]
abandon[...]
return [...]

100

DOM EDMOND OBRECHT:
MONK of GETHSEMANI, CITIZEN of the WORLD
1898-1935

E VERY EPIC HAS ITS HERO, THE COURAGEOUS INDI-vidual who intercedes in a crisis, and by virtue of intellect, integrity and sheer force of personality leads those he loves from chaos to order.

Dom Edmond Obrecht is that kind of hero. A big-hearted, robust Alsatian, he looms larger than life in Gethsemani's history. His 200-pound frame gave him an imposing air of authority that his talent and character confirmed. He was abbot for 37 years, a span of time equal to the combined tenures of his two predecessors.

His regime began at the turn of the century, spanned a world war, endured an economic depression and, most importantly, presided over the transformation of Gethsemani from struggling French foundation to thriving American monastery. He had never stepped foot in Kentucky at the time he took charge of its only abbey, but Dom Edmond did not remain a stranger for long.

Though he spoke several European languages fluently and retained a fondness for continental customs, he insisted from the start that his monks speak English exclusively. For a community that was still composed chiefly of French, German and Irish monks, this edict reflected the new abbot's fervent desire to rid Gethsemani of its cloudy Old-World image. It was time Gethsemani found its rightful place in the 20th-century American landscape, and Dom Edmond was determined to have that happen under his watch.

WHY AND HOW DID HE ATTAIN HIS LEGENDARY STATUS? Timing and expectations had something to do with it. Dom Edmond rode boldly into Gethsemani's darkest hour, a white knight from a far-off land, armed with the weapon few can resist – the salvo of a second chance. Nearly forsaken by the Order under its previous admin-istration, now Gethsemani was sent a leader with ties to the upper echelons of the Catholic hierar-chy and a record for getting things done.

OPPOSITE: *Portrait of Dom Edmond Obrecht.*
ABOVE: *Early view of entrance to the abbey church.*
RIGHT: *A gold and ivory chalice given to Dom Edmond in honor of his Golden Jubilee.*

All this being said, it was Dom Edmond's nature and temperament, above all, that won him the confidence of his monks. Their affection for him and their loyalty, which is amply evident in all that was written about him in letters and official records of the time, is what inspired the astonishing turnabout in the abbey's spiritual and material fortunes.

Central casting could not have sent a better man to do the job of resurrecting Gethsemani from its fallen state. Dom Edmond was, in the words of those who knew him, warm, witty, organized, strong-willed, sophisticated, decisive, politically intuitive, virile, sensitive, sociable, a listener, a brilliant conversationalist, exuberant, affectionate, tenacious, a good money manager, a good judge of people, and a born leader. Not to put too fine a point on it, but he seemed to possess all that his predecessor had lacked. Who among the shell-shocked troops of Gethsemani would not welcome with open arms such a captain?

His legacy, however, transcends kind words from his contemporaries. His contributions were significant and lasting.

An avid collector of historical artifacts before becoming abbot, Dom Edmond put his hobby to work at Gethsemani and amassed an astonishing collection of Medieval books and rare Cistercian manuscripts that have grown only more valuable with time. He is also responsible for the acquisition of a vast and varied library of 40,000 volumes, bequeathed to the abbey by his friend, Monsignor Leonard Batz of Milwaukee.

IN 1973, GETHSEMANI PERMANENTLY LOANED DOM EDMOND'S COLLECTION OF RARE MEDIEVAL MANUSCRIPTS AND INCUNABULA (BOOKS PRINTED BEFORE 1501) TO THE INSTITUTE OF CISTERCIAN STUDIES AT WESTERN MICHIGAN UNIVERSITY AT KALAMAZOO.

THE COLLECTION CONSISTS OF 37 BOUND VOLUMES, 17 UNBOUND FILES AND 58 INCUNABULA. THERE ARE ALSO HUNDREDS OF VOLUMES

OF INTEREST TO SCHOLARS AND OTHER RESEARCHERS OF THE PERIOD. THE WORKS OF BERNARD OF CLAIRVAUX ARE HEAVILY REPRESENTED IN THE COLLECTION. SHOWN AT LEFT, A 16TH-CENTURY ANTIPHONARY DEPICTING THE STONING OF ST. STEPHEN.

THE ABBACY OF DOM EDMOND

1898: Dom Edmond is named superior of Gethsemani in March and elected abbot October 10.

1900: U.S. Census records 12 million Roman Catholics, twice the number of next largest denomination, Methodists.

1901: Trappist Post Office is established in the abbey gatehouse, with Father Frederic Dunne as its first postmaster.

1904: Marie Curie discovers two new radioactive elements: radium and polonium.

1905: Swiss physicist Albert Einstein introduces the equation E=mc2.

1905-6: Dom Edmond travels through Africa and Europe visiting monasteries.

1909: Stained-glass windows made in Munich replace plain glass in abbey church.

1911: *The S.S. Titantic* of the White Star line sinks on her maiden voyage.

1917: U.S. declares war on Germany.

1925: Dom Edmond's health begins to decline.

1926: Dom Edmond visits Carmel of Lisieux for the first time.

1930: Virginia Woolf boosts cause of feminism with publication of *A Room of One's Own*.

1931: Gethsemani has 80 men, including 13 novices and three oblates.

1933: Hitler is named Chancellor, then seizes power in Germany.

1934: Dom Edmond is anointed on November 13 (his 83rd birthday).

1935: Dom Edmond dies on January 4 after 37 years as abbot of Gethsemani.

ABOVE: *Dom Edmond in the gatehouse museum, which he filled with items he collected during his travels.*

BELOW: *A reliquary containing relics of saints.*

RIGHT: *The monastic library, named for Monsignor Leonard Batz of Milwaukee, who donated 40,000 books.*

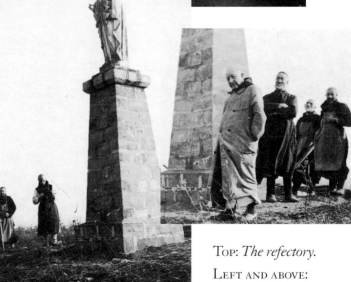

Dom Edmond transformed the face of the abbey from its interior chambers to the perimeter of the property, installing stained-glass windows made by Munich's finest artisans in the church and building a wall seven feet high and 6,000 feet in length to enclose the monastic land that was off-limits to the public.

He was the first abbot in America to allow women to enter the monastic cloister on visits. He initiated organized weekend retreats for outsiders (men only). He established an enduring connection with the sisters of St. Thérèse of Lisieux. He forged important ties with political leaders inside and outside the church. He knew how to entertain in grand style, as newspaper accounts of his various jubilees and gala celebrations attest. In the end, perhaps the accomplishment most appreciated by his monks was Dom Edmond's adamant refusal to rebuild Gethsemani College after it burned in 1912.

TOP: *The refectory.*
LEFT AND ABOVE: *The statue of St. Joseph erected on the site of Gethsemani College after the school burned in 1912. Dom Edmond (inset) chose not to rebuild.*

ABOVE: *Dom Edmond at his roll-top desk*.
LEFT: *Community portrait of Dom Edmond and the lay brothers*.
BELOW: *One of Dom Edmond's vestments, sewn with gold thread*.

YET, FOR ALL THAT, HIS LIFE WAS A PARADOX, a contradiction in terms. For a member of a contemplative order, Dom Edmond led an extraordinarily active life. In truth, for many years, he lived like a missionary rather than a monk. Before coming to Gethsemani, he spent more than a dozen years at Tre Fontane, an abbey outside Rome, where he knew and mingled with key leaders of the Catholic Church. He then moved to New York City, his home base for the several years he spent as the official Trappist fund raiser in America. He learned English there, working in an urban mission run by Father William Daugherty, a priest who would become a lifelong friend.

Within four years of his election as abbot, he was spending years at a stretch away from the abbey, traveling throughout Europe and Africa, visiting Trappist houses, checking out their health and diagnosing prob-

lems for the Order. He spent most of the years between 1904 and 1907 in South Africa, for example, studying the difficulties of a new abbey known as the Marianhill Mission. For years he would wrestle with the dilemma he found there – contemplative monks actively engaged in converting Africans to Catholicism. He was also given responsibility for houses in the U.S., Canada, Europe and Asia. Beginning in 1911, he made an extensive three-year tour of the world, from Ireland to China, Korea, Japan and Hawaii, with annual digressions to France for Trappist meetings. In his later years, he rarely missed an opportunity to visit the Carmelites at Lisieux, with whom he had established a trans-Atlantic correspondence. He sometimes found time to visit his hometown of Stotzheim in Alsace, and tried to stop by Rome, when possible, a place he thought of as his "second home." So dear were his memories of his time at Tre Fontane that 40 years later, when Mussolini's fascist government confiscated the Trappist residence in Rome, Dom Edmond saw to it that Gethsemani paid for a new one to replace it.

At Dom Edmond's death, a reporter for *The Record*, Louisville's archdiocesan newspaper, described the 83-year-old abbot as "a citizen of the world . . . versed in its politics . . . a man of learning, a lover of arts and letters, a scholar, and a keen observer of men and times."

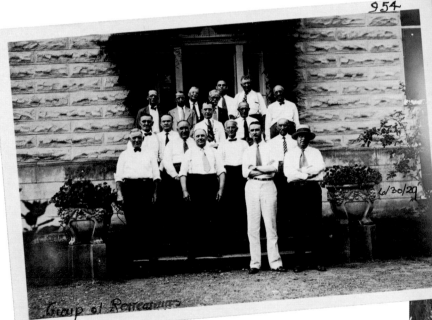

A CAREFUL READING OF DOM EDMOND'S TENURE CANnot help but beg a question, however. How did he accomplish so much at Gethsemani when he was so seldom present? An official biography published two years after the abbot's death explains this feat by citing the many factors described above – plus one more. Namely, Father Frederic Dunne, Dom Edmond's prior. The secret of the abbot's success was, in part, the work of the man he left in charge.

Fr. Frederic ran Gethsemani during his abbot's frequent absences. His almost daily letters to Dom

LEFT: *Dom Edmond initiated weekend retreats for groups of lay men, such as these.* TOP RIGHT: *A view of the retreat area in the south wing of the monastery.* ABOVE: *Dom Edmond with a visitor in the front garden.*

110

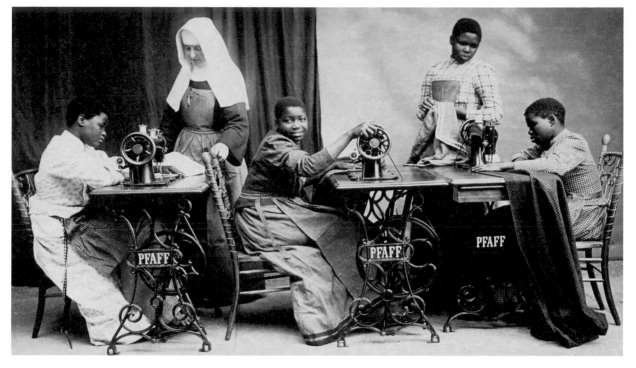

In 1879, in an uncharacteristic move for the Order, a Trappist foundation was made in Natal, South Africa, for the purpose of evangelizing the villagers. It was called Marianhill. From the start, some questioned the notion of contemplative monks working at such an active missionary life. In 1904 Dom Edmond was named administrator of the rapidly expanding Marianhill. Ultimately the monastery was closed and its mission taken over by an independent order. These 1907 photographs chronicle the Trappist years at Marianhill.

Edmond, which were salvaged by Thomas Merton and now reside in the abbey archives, testify to Fr. Frederic's affection for his abbot and also to his own leadership abilities. While Dom Edmond endured the physical rigors of South Africa's extreme climate and tortuous road travel, Fr. Frederic was in Nelson County trying to keep his monks from succumbing to Kentucky's unrelenting summer heat, particularly as they carried out the abbot's endless construction projects. Fr. Frederic, for his part, was proving he could inspire both choir monk and lay brother to meet the challenge of Dom Edmond's high expectations.

In letter after letter, Fr. Frederic accounts for every cement block added to the enclosure wall, every misstep proclaimed and punished, every monk with a toothache, every good neighbor's death, every harvest of red clover. Fr. Frederic's tone is always efficient and light-hearted, no matter what the news is. And it can be, on occasion, quite alarming: for example, an unexpected encounter with moonshiners at work in the woods of the monastery. More often it is a litany of hard work, as described in the following letter penned by Fr. Frederic on a day in late August.

Everything goes on in the usual way at home. The work is the same: making blocks for the enclosure wall, laying foundations. Those not necessary for this are spraying the vines and, this afternoon, digging some potatoes for supper. The novices are destroying iron weeds today. Yesterday they

Dom Edmond's prior, Father Frederic Dunne, walking behind the abbey church.

were cleaning out weeds from the corn, a job which, Deo Gratias, is very well advanced.

For 34 years, Fr. Frederic served Dom Edmond as his prior, gaining valuable experience and the respect of his community. At Dom Edmond's death, there was little question that Fr. Frederic would be his able successor.

DOM EDMOND'S DEATH, when it came, was no surprise. His lengthy and often arduous travels had taken a toll. He had a history of heart attacks, many of them suffered on the road. Diabetes exacerbated his health problems. Then, in 1933, he was hurt in a car accident not far from the monastery. An injury to his leg, considered minor at first, eventually led his doctor to consider amputation. Dom Edmond prayed to St. Thérèse of Lisieux when he heard the diagnosis, and later attributed his sudden, inexplicable and complete recovery to his favorite saint's intercession. Even so, he was never quite the same after the collision.

In 1934, he was hospitalized in Louisville with cardiac symptoms. Later that year, he agreed to visit Our Lady of the Valley, a monastery in Rhode Island for which he shared responsibility. The trip proved to be too much. Back home, he made his last appearance before the community on November 1. On November 13, his 83rd birthday, he asked to be anointed. He died on January 4, 1935.

Commonweal, the Catholic magazine, ran an article

after his death in which the author, Michael Williams, told a simple story that shed light on the philosophy and character of Gethsemani's preeminent, paradoxical abbot, Dom Edmond Obrecht:

In his cell at Gethsemani, on his desk, there was a statue of Our Lady of Peace in a sort of shrine, the supporting columns of which were two shells brought back by the old soldier monk from some battlefield in France after the world war.

The image fits. Dom Edmond was, indeed, a realist who intuitively understood the cold, hard workings of a broken world. But he was also a true believer in the pursuit of peace and love, the Trappist's vocation.

ABOVE: *A view of the monastic cemetery.*
RIGHT: *One of the last photographs taken of Dom Edmond.*
BELOW: *The official funeral card at his death.*

113

ABOVE: *A banquet in the cloister for Governor Augustus Willson and guests, 1911.* BELOW: *Dom Edmond's leather document case.*

GETHSEMANI OPENS SOME DOORS, CLOSES OTHERS

June 7, 1899: Gethsemani's Golden Jubilee begins. Brother Antoninus Dumont, the only founder still living, carries the wooden cross that Dom Eutropius brought from Melleray. A "women's banquet" is held and hundreds picnic on the lawn.

June 5, 1901: Gethsemani receives Rome's permission to open its cloister to a female visitor, a first for an Ameri-

REFUGEES DRIVEN FROM FRANCE--COME TO GETHSEMANI.

THE REFUGEES FROM FRANCE. THE REV. FATHER EDMUND O. OBRECHT, ABBOT OF GETHSEMANI, IS IN THE CENTER.

PAX INTRANTIBUS

NEW HAVEN, NELSON CO., KY., THURSDAY, JUNE 18, 1903.

The Refugee Trappist Who are at Gethsemani Abbey.

THE TRAPPIST REFUGEES FROM FRANCE.

Right Rev. Father Abbot O'Brecht is in the center of the group.

REFUGEE MONKS REACH KENTUCKY.

Seventeen, Recently Expelled From Their Home in France, Arrive Under the Guidance of Father Obrecht, Abbot of Gethsemani.

ABOVE: A monk in the entrance of the old gatehouse.

LEFT: Newspaper coverage of the arrival of French refugee monks.

BELOW LEFT: A postcard captioned "Front view with shrine of the B. Virgin."

Abbey of Gethsemani

Front view with shrine of the B. Virgin.

can Trappist monastery. Gov. J.C.W. Beckham and his wife arrive to the college band playing *Hail to the Chief* and *My Old Kentucky Home.*

1903: Gethsemani welcomes 17 exiled monks from Fontgombault on June 10. The French refugees set up a provisional monastery at Mount Olivet and make a foundation in Oregon the following year. In 1910, the foundation closes. Three monks join Gethsemani, but most go to Our Lady of the Lake at Oka, Canada.

1912: Gethsemani College burns to the ground on March 1; Dom Edmond decides not to rebuild. A statue of St. Joseph is moved to the site.

1920: Gethsemani discontinues housing of "penitent" priests, a custom that provided rooms for priests charged with misconduct. Dom Edmond replaces that program with weekend retreats for lay men.

May 21, 1924: Gethsemani renovates church to celebrate its Diamond Jubilee with a Mass and grand banquet. Guests include the archbishop of New Orleans, bishops of many dioceses and abbots of Melleray and other monasteries. Hundreds wait outside when the church fills up. Patrons donate $3,725 to help cover expenses.

THE HOUSE THAT OBRECHT BUILT
(and REPLACED, RENOVATED, TORE DOWN and REBUILT...)

Opposite: *Dom Edmond and visitors observe the building of the new cloister.* Above: *A view of the front garden and new gatehouse with the avenue in the background.* Left: *A monk in the front garden.* Far Left: *A smoothing plane used by Gethsemani monks.*

117

1284–
7/24/32

1898: Hen house is built.

1900: Fire destroys cow barn but cows are saved.

1904: New cow barn is completed with windmill. Livestock at the time consists of 7 horses, 9 mules, 43 cows, 20 heifers, 33 calves, 3 bulls, 43 hogs, 2 boars, 14 pigs, 39 sheep, 32 lambs, 7 goats and 3 kids, for a market value of $3,751.

Insects destroy avenue of elms leading to gatehouse. The 86 trees, planted in four rows, had grown from French saplings brought over by the founders in 1848. They are replaced by 78 sweet gums supplied by the Louisville Parks Commission.

PAX INTRANTIBUS

TRAPPIST P.O

Opposite top: *The front entrance looking up the avenue.*

Opposite bottom: *The chicken yard.* Above: *The original gatehouse.*

Right: *The Post Office at Gethsemani.*

Gethsemani Barns

The Abbey of Gethsemani. View from North.

ABOVE: *A view of the Shops Building and an early postcard.*
OPPOSITE, TOP TO BOTTOM: *Construction of the new gate-house, the preau with grape vines in the snow, and a postcard of the front entrance showing the cut stone façade.*

1907: Work is finished on dairy, forge, shoe shop, laundry, bindery, print shop and wine press. Red-brick facing on church is covered with a simulated cut-stone facing. Vineyard expansion begins. Wire fence replaces wood rail fence on farm. Cistern is built on "Nally Hill" across highway. Shops Building is completed.

1909: Stained-glass windows from Munich, Germany, are installed in church.

1910: Gatehouse goes up in flames.

Exterior Entrance to Church,
Our Lady of Gethsemani, Trappist P. O., Ky.

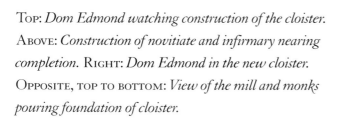

Top: *Dom Edmond watching construction of the cloister.*
Above: *Construction of novitiate and infirmary nearing completion.* Right: *Dom Edmond in the new cloister.*
Opposite, top to bottom: *View of the mill and monks pouring foundation of cloister.*

1911: A concrete, fireproof gatehouse replaces old one and houses Post Office, store, parlors, museum, guest rooms, paint shop, storerooms and sleeping quarters for two porters. Mosaic floor and stained-glass windows are installed in cloister.

1914: Excavation begins for a cistern near mill.

1915: New woodshed built to replace the one torn down for monastery addition.

1916: Work is finished on addition, which includes new novitiate and infirmary.

1917: A concrete silo is added to the cow barn.

1923: Library roof is repaired after damage by tornado.

ABOVE: *The chapter room.*

RIGHT: *A view of the secular chapel.*

OPPOSITE: *The monastic wall, the lay brothers' section of the choir and an early postcard of the front entrance.*

1924: Main altar of church is redone. Hardwood floor is laid. Enamel stations are added. Plaster partition separating monks and public is removed; a series of new Munich stained-glass windows and new organ are installed. Philadelphia's Cardinal Dougherty donates replica of Titian Assumption window.

1925: A shed is built for carts and wagons.

1927: Hardwood floors are installed in chapter room.

1928: New sheep barn is built.

1930: Work begins on cement-block enclosure wall that will be 6,000 feet long and 7 feet high. Monks make their own cement blocks, dig trenches and quarry stone.

1931: Enclosure wall is finished October 22.

Dom Frederic Dunne:
Exploring New Frontiers
1935-1948

For thirty-seven years, Gethsemani's identity was bound up in the personality of its colorful Alsatian abbot. It didn't matter that Dom Edmond spent much of his time thousands of miles from the abbey, crisscrossing Europe, Asia and Africa, living a far different life from that of his monks. He was a commanding figure, impossible to ignore even in his absence. By the time of his death in 1935, Dom Edmond Obrecht *was* Gethsemani in the mind of the public.

Under the new abbot, Dom Frederic Dunne, this image would change. Gethsemani would no longer reflect the character or the vision of a single monk. When people thought about the abbey, Dom Frederic wanted them to think about the *life* there, not the *leader*. As Dom Edmond's prior for three decades, he had plenty of experience running a monastery without calling attention to himself. He did not intend to change now that he occupied the abbot's office.

Like his predecessor, however, Dom Frederic believed it was essential to get the word out about Gethsemani, if for no other reason than as a recruitment tool. Under Dom Edmond, the community hosted public events that made newspaper headlines and treated government officials to guided tours of the enclosure. Certainly these efforts helped spread the message of monastic life to a nation unfamiliar with it, but they also placed enormous strain on the community. Dom Frederic knew first-hand what a toll these public events could take on the contemplative life. He also knew ban-

Top: *A document, signed by Pius XI, bestowing on Dom Frederic the honor of wearing the caped vestment known as the Cappa Magna.* Bottom: *Governor Albert "Happy" Chandler and family visiting Dom Frederic.* Opposite: *Monks reading in Gethsemani's Batz Library.*

quets and guided tours did not reach many ordinary Americans, the group that he felt needed contact with Gethsemani. He was convinced there was a far less disruptive way to reach a significantly larger audience.

Books were what he had in mind. Dom Frederic, from childhood, was a voracious reader and an admirer, in particular, of poetry. He believed in the power of the written word and sensed the time was right to use it to the monastery's advantage. He had reason to trust his instincts in this arena. Before entering Gethsemani in 1894, Dom Frederic worked several years with his father, Hugh Dunne, in the printing and book-binding business. He was keenly aware of how vast an audience one well-written book could reach.

All Dom Frederic needed to make his plan work, then, was a writer. He was blessed with two: Father

Raymond Flanagan and Father Louis Merton, who wrote under his secular name, Thomas Merton. Both were prolific authors. Between them, they published countless pamphlets and more than 70 books, introducing Gethsemani to millions of readers who might never have heard its name otherwise. The abbot mentored both monks, encouraging them to write in a variety of genres.

Fr. Raymond concentrated on historical novels which he often based on notable Trappist characters and events. His romantic storytelling style and his Hollywood titles *(God Goes to Murderer's Row* and *The Man Who Got Even With God)* were popular with Catholic readers of the 1950s. He also authored a series of "recruiting" pamphlets.

Fr. Louis, on the other hand, covered the literary waterfront. He made an international name for himself and the abbey by publishing hundreds of articles and some 50 books, including collections of poetry and political essays, works of theology, spirituality, biography, criticism and history, personal journals and a blockbuster autobiography, *The Seven Storey Mountain.* In 1947 alone, Fr. Louis had 12 writing projects in the works. It became clear over time that books not only got out the message but brought in the money.

In the end, Dom Frederic's abbacy would be identified far less with him than with the image of Trappist life created by his two monk-writers. In the years following the publication of Merton's hugely popular autobiography, it's unlikely that many Americans could have named the abbot of Gethsemani – but many were aware of the way of life there. What pleased Dom Frederic most, however, was the fact that record numbers of those Americans were now knocking at Gethsemani's

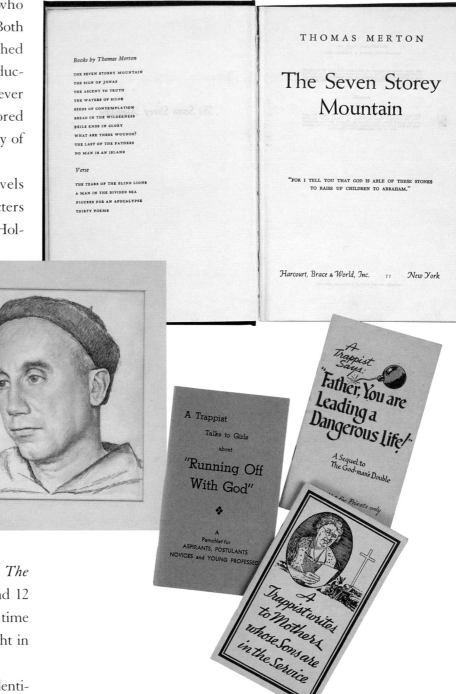

TOP: *Thomas Merton's bestseller, "The Seven Storey Mountain."* CENTER: *Study for a portrait of Merton by Victor Hammer.* BOTTOM: *Inspirational pamphlets written by Father Raymond Flanagan.* OPPOSITE: *Dom Frederic (circled) as a choir monk early in Dom Edmond's abbacy. Dom Edmond is in the front row at left.*

As Professed

gatehouse door, asking permission to enter the austere life they had come to know in books. This had been his hope all along.

In *The Seven Mountains of Thomas Merton,* biographer Michael Mott describes an encounter that took place between Dom Frederic and Fr. Louis three months before *The Seven Storey Mountain* hit bookstores and began its steady march to bestsellerdom. Dom Frederic had summoned Fr. Louis to his office to give him an advance copy he had received. As Fr. Louis later recalled, the abbot seemed as exhilarated by the book as he did.

And why wouldn't Dom Frederic find this moment exciting? He had read the book. Surely he felt the power of the story told within its pages. He may have known intuitively, as he handed over the freshly bound volume

that day, that this was a book that would change life at Gethsemani for generations to come.

What neither abbot nor monk knew, however, was that Dom Frederic would not live to see that change take place. The book that catapulted Gethsemani from backwoods obscurity to teeming Trappist monastery and can't-miss tourist site was released to bookstores on October 4, 1948 – two months after Dom Frederic's death.

A SHARED AFFECTION FOR BOOKS WAS NOT ALL THAT Fr. Louis and his abbot had in common. They each had lost their mothers at an early age: Dom Frederic at seven, when his mother died giving birth to a younger brother; Fr. Louis at six, when his mother succumbed to stomach cancer. Oddly enough, Dom Frederic shared this same sad personal history with *his* abbot: Dom Edmond had lost his mother soon after he was born.

For Dom Frederic, this early loss meant being raised primarily by a loving sister, Katherine, who was eight years older than he. Hugh Dunne traveled a great deal after his wife's death, and Katherine took on the role of parent in his absence. Dom Frederic was 20 when he decided to leave the family behind in Florida and enter Gethsemani.

He arrived in the summer of 1894, just before the Gethsemani College scandal broke. Dom Edmond put him in charge of the school after the principal was fired, and then added the job of prior to his responsibilities in 1901. He remained in the prior's post until August 1933, when Dom Edmond made him confessor of the novices. In his biography of Dom Frederic, *The Less Traveled Road,* Fr. Raymond writes that he greatly appreciated being relieved of the prior's job after performing it for 32 years. Dom Frederic considered the days that followed "the happiest period of his life," according to his biographer. But the new job and the time it freed up for prayer turned out to be short-lived. Dom Edmond died in January 1935. On February 6, Dom Frederic – the man

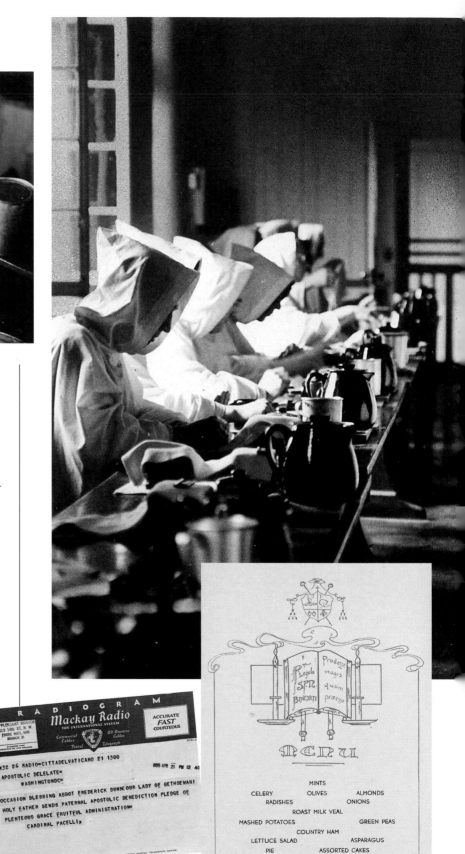

THE ABBACY OF DOM FREDERIC

1935: Gethsemani elects Dom Frederic Dunne as first American abbot of Trappist monastery.

1937: Great Ohio Valley flood displaces 200,000.

1939: Some Trappist monks are sent to death camps while others manage to join the Resistance, as Nazis close or occupy monasteries across Europe.

1940: First peacetime military draft in U.S. history begins.

1941: Thomas Merton enters Gethsemani December 10.

1942: John Paul Merton is baptized during visit to Gethsemani, just months before his death in wartime raid in Mannheim in 1943.

1944: Founders of Gethsemani's first daughterhouse depart for Conyers, Georgia.

1945: Soviet troops liberate Auschwitz.

1946: Father James Fox is elected abbot of Holy Ghost Abbey.

1947: A second foundation is made in Utah.

1948: Dom Frederic dies August 4 on his way to visit foundation in Georgia.

who had run the monastery during Dom Edmond's long and frequent absences – was elected the fifth abbot of Gethsemani.

His election was historic: he became the first American abbot of a Trappist monastery. It was a moment of transition for the abbey. Yet Dom Frederic would prove to be as unbending as the sternest of his French predecessors when it came to The Rule.

If there is a honeymoon for new abbots, as there often is for elected leaders in the secular world, Dom Frederic was deprived of his. Within days, the monastery was hit hard by a Spanish influenza epidemic. The first death came nine days after Dom Frederic's election. Ten days later, six more were dead. It was not until May 1, with his men on the mend and Kentucky spring in full bloom, that Dom Frederic received his abbatial blessing.

FOR HIS FIRST MAJOR DECISION AS ABBOT FIFTY YEARS earlier, Dom Edward Chaix-Bourbon chose to elevate the boys' boarding school to the status of a college. One of Dom Edmond's first steps in 1898 was to plan a public celebration of Gethsemani's 50th anniversary. Both men looked to the outside world to set the tone for their abbacies.

Dom Frederic's first effort was an internal one, aimed at reforming the fabric of life at Gethsemani. He set out to restore a literal interpretation of the Trappist rule. He did not wish to impose it, however; he asked the community to vote on it. Over the years, "mitigations"– the monastic term for official modifications – had softened some rules, taking the sting out of the more rigorous requirements. Dom Frederic asked Gethsemani's monks to forget those mitigations and follow the rules to the letter.

The community took many votes on the mitigations, always supporting the abbot's requests. Consequently day-to-day life at the abbey became considerably tougher. For example, the monks gave up the small portion of extra food they had been receiving in the mornings during the Trappist fast that lasts a good part of each year. Mitigations had permitted six ounces of bread with an occasional dish of fruit or serving of butter. After the vote, however, the community returned to the stricter portion of two ounces of bread with a cup of the "common drink of the country." In Europe that drink was wine. In the U.S., according to Dom

Frederic, it was a barley beverage that *looked* like but did not *taste* like coffee.

There were other retrenchments, including the withdrawal of two privileges Dom Frederic considered excessive: the freedom to sleep 30 minutes later than usual on mornings after the community had risen a half-hour early for feast days; and permission to share a meal with relatives during the one family visit allotted to each monk annually. In his personal remembrances of Dom Frederic, Fr. Louis had noted that the abbot was even disdainful of the lighter-weight habit his monks wore in summer, claiming "it wouldn't kill us to wear wool."

On the other hand, Dom Frederic was a liberating force for change in terms of the intellectual life of the community. He opened up the library to choir monks on Sunday afternoons. He reorganized the seminary by authorizing a strong academic curriculum and putting in charge a monk who had run a major Canadian monastery before entering Gethsemani. He did his part to squelch the anti-intellectual attitudes fostered by some older monks.

Whether or not it was Dom Frederic's doing, the community began to grow. Well before Fr. Louis and Fr. Raymond nudged the recruitment process with their books, the numbers were increasing. When Dom Frederic was elected, there were 68 men in the community. A year later, there were 82. At the start of World War II, the number rose to 126; at its end, it was up to 145. Before he died, Dom Frederic would have a house so full that he would easily spare 70 of his men to make Gethsemani's first foundations in rural Georgia and the mountains of Utah. Many of those who would make the abbey their home were men who had witnessed the trauma of battle in the armed forces and now felt alienated from a postwar culture that, to them, seemed empty and lacking in all direction and purpose. The contemplative life offered a welcome alternative.

FOUNDATIONS AND REGULATIONS WERE NOT THE ONLY big changes during Dom Frederic's years as abbot. Physically, the monastery experienced yet another metamorphosis. In 1944, a young man with experience in the field of architecture entered Gethsemani. Brother Clement, as John Dorsey would be known for the 25 years he was a lay brother there, was Dom Frederic's point man for the massive and long-term construction project that – years after the abbot was dead – would bring the monastic complex into the modern world.

LAY BRETHREN 1936

Dorsey was joined in his work by four other talented members of the community, including a Catholic University-educated architect (Brother Giles Naughton); a Chicago commercial artist (Brother Ephrem Cole); a former World War II Seabee (Father Anastasius); and a builder who had worked, among other places, for AT&T in Chicago (Brother Claude). In an interview in 1997, nearly 30 years after he had left the monastery and married, Dorsey recalled how the project began under Dom Frederic. As he remembers, he was finishing his novitiate as a lay brother when the abbot asked him to create a "plot plan" of the monastic grounds.

OPPOSITE: Cells in Gethsemani's dormitory. ABOVE: Dom Frederic with the lay brothers. LEFT: John Dorsey, former Brother Clement, the cellarer, with Gertie the cow.

"When I brought that to him, he said the first thing he would like to do is build the horse barn because the old one was pretty well dilapidated," Dorsey recalled.

But Dom Frederic had made up his mind that the barn should be built in the middle of what was then a vineyard. This surprised Dorsey because he knew Gethsemani had made its own wine, for drinking and for use

A state-issued certificate, in Dom Frederic's name, identified Gethsemani as a legitimate producer of hemp, or "marihuana." For several

years, the monastery cultivated the crop, whose fiber was used in the production of rope and cloth.

at Mass, from the earliest days of the foundation. What he didn't know was that the vineyards never supplied the monks with enough grapes. They had to buy from other growers to fortify their wine. Dom Frederic believed it would be more economical in the long run to buy the wine they needed and surrender the romantic notion of making their own wine. With no further ado, the vineyard was plowed under and the horse barn erected. In the process, Dorsey had his first glimpse of Dom Frederic's pragmatic side and his willingness to leave the "Old World" Gethsemani behind.

Under Dom Frederic's supervision, his monks opened up more space for storerooms and workshops by excavating beneath the monastery buildings and constructing basement rooms. They put up a 160-foot tower with a 30,000-gallon tank to hold water from the artificial lake they created in the woods across the road from the monastery. They built a new novitiate wing and a fire-proof horse barn. Dom Frederic was also responsible for introducing electric lights, telephones and a fire-fighting system.

Dorsey, who would take charge of an even more ambitious building program under the next abbot, recalls Dom Frederic telling him that there were really only two lessons a monk had to learn: "to do as you're told and to do as you're told."

Obedience, a hallmark of early Cistercian religious life, was as important in Dom Frederic's day as it was at the time of Citeaux. Under Dom Frederic, the daily experience of being a monk was in truth not too different from that of the founders. It was primitive, arduous and highly restricted. It made sense, in the context of the times, that those who had survived the deprivations of the battlefield would be among those most attracted to monasticism, despite the hardships inherent in that life.

ABOVE RIGHT: *The tool that applied the official seal of Gethsemani.*

Hot water, at the time, was available only for shaving, which occurred weekly on a designated day. In winter, a monk's habit typically consisted of layers of thick wool robes and aprons heaped over more layers of coarse duck underclothes – an outfit that could weigh up to 20 pounds. Although the community switched to lighter-weight fabrics for the remainder of the year, the monks' bulky habits were still ill-suited for Kentucky summers. Year-round, the men were expected to sleep in their habits. They could mail out letters four times a year, only on designated religious holidays. There were similar restrictions on reading incoming letters. All mail, coming in and going out, was read and censored before reaching its destination.

Mistakes were dealt with harshly in the Chapter of Faults. This ancient monastic practice that became a Cistercian institution during the Middle Ages was carried out at mandatory meetings where individual monks publicly "proclaimed" others or themselves for lapses in conduct. Penances, or punishments, were handed out by the abbot. They ranged from eating one's supper while sitting on the floor, to lying face down in front of the refectory door while others filed inside.

Brother Kevin Shine, who entered Gethsemani in 1942 and died in 1998, liked to tell the story of his refusal, at first, to proclaim others. "It wasn't my style," he recalled. "Then somebody proclaimed me for not doing it. So I had to proclaim someone, and I did. But it never went down well with me. I was sure happy when that disappeared." The practice ended in the 1960s in the wake of Vatican II reforms.

Life was harsher certainly, but also less complicated. Br. Giles entered Gethsemani in 1941. He recalled that the work was simple and straightforward: farming, gar-

dening, tending the fields and woods. The cheese and bread made in the monks' bakery were sold mainly in neighboring towns and in the gatehouse gift shop. There was no mail-order business, no open door to women, no speaking without permission.

A crude sign language made it possible to convey basic information when necessary – be it an exchange between two monks working the same job, or an aside that simply couldn't be suppressed. As one monk who lived through that era puts it, there are many ways to tell your neighbor to go to hell without uttering a syllable.

To help newcomers acclimate to the exceptional way

of life they had chosen, each novice was assigned a "guardian angel," a custom that still exists today at Gethsemani. One duty of the angel was to teach the new arrival how to sign. Daily vocabulary testing was part of the process. Br. Kevin was Dorsey's angel, but the older monk had entered Gethsemani as a middle-aged man and had never mastered the use of signs himself. So Dorsey turned to Br. Giles for help. He still remembers the gesture his tutor would make whenever he failed a vocabulary test. He would flash him the sign for "thick."

DOM FREDERIC HAD entered Gethsemani at a time when some in the order had worried that the American community would not survive. By 1943, the problem had reversed itself. Now there was concern that Gethsemani would burst at the seams with so many men crowded into the house.

To Dom Frederic, the solution was obvious. It was time for the monks of Gethsemani to do what the monks of Melleray had done before them – make a foundation. Years before the Civil War, several American bishops had invited Dom Eutropius to establish a daughterhouse in their dioceses. He had declined, wanting to put his own house in order before founding a new one. Dom Frederic had received his share of invitations too, and had put off making any decisions until he could consult with his superiors in France.

But that was impossible in 1943. War was raging in Europe. The order had not held a General Chapter since 1938. Nazis were occupying – or had closed down – Trappist monasteries across Europe. Some monks had escaped imprisonment and joined the Resistance Army.

Others were not so fortunate. Monks from Engelszell monastery in Austria, for example, were sent to Dachau, where they died.

Contact with Rome, then, was virtually impossible. If permission for a foundation were to be secured, it would have to come from the Apostolic Delegate in Washington. And though Dom Frederic's overcrowding problems were minor by comparison with the troubles facing other Trappist abbeys at the time, he couldn't ignore them. There was something else at work, too. The Cistercian cycle of life – an abbey's instinctive urge to give birth to a daughterhouse – was as old as Citeaux and could not be ignored.

In December 1943, the abbot investigated several potential monastery sites in Georgia that had come to his attention. He settled on a 1,464-acre plantation about 30 miles south of Atlanta and six miles west of a town called Conyers. On February 7, 1944, after obtaining the necessary approval from the Apostolic Delegate in Washington, Dom Frederic bought the land, known as Honey Creek Plantation, for $45,000.

J. Leslie Ray, a contractor from New Haven, Kentucky, was hired to turn a big brick barn on the property into a makeshift dormitory and chapel shared with chickens and cows. Now all that was necessary was for Dom Frederic to decide who would make the foundation that would be christened Our Lady of the Holy Ghost and renamed Holy Spirit in the 1960s. While Dom Frederic compiled that list and worked out the details, the new foundation was kept secret from the community.

In *The Waters of Siloe,* Fr. Louis suggests word leaked out nonetheless. He reports that signs were flashing – fast and furious – in the days leading up to Dom Frederic's announcement. On March 19, the feast of St. Joseph, what had been rumored became real. Coincidentally, this was also the day when Fr. Louis, the man whose words would lead to even more overcrowding in years to come, made his simple profession.

Before a silent community, Dom Frederic read the names of 20 monks who would head out with him for Georgia two days later. Their departure date was also well timed: March 21 was the feast of St. Benedict, and also the anniversary of the founding of Citeaux.

When that day came, the departing group said good-bye to their brothers at the gate, then left the monastery in a cavalcade of cars. They carried with them a replica of the cross that Dom Eutropius brought

Top: *The founders of Gethsemani's first foundation at Conyers, Georgia.* Above: *Dom Frederic during construction of the monastery of the Holy Ghost.*

from Melleray. At nearby Gethsemani Station, they boarded an overnight train bound for Atlanta. They sang Compline in a train aisle that night, and Matins and Lauds the next morning.

When they arrived in Atlanta, they transferred baggage from train to truck, then climbed into cars that drove them the rest of the way. It was midday when the caravan arrived at the monks' new home – and it was raining. Rather than dampen the spirits of the men, the

AT THE MILL

GOING TO WORK

rain must have served as a bittersweet reminder of the history they bore with them to Georgia. In 1848, rain had fallen on the founders of Gethsemani, first as they left Melleray and again when they pulled into Bardstown. For this particular branch of the Trappist family tree, rainfall surely was a sign of God's blessing.

Weather – mostly extremes of it – continued to play an important role in the drama that was the first year of Holy Ghost's life. Heavy rains fell that spring, as the monks worked the fields. The searing Georgia heat beat down all summer as they felled trees for lumber and

began construction of their pine-board monastery. Despite these stumbling blocks, the monks completed their work in time to move out of the hayloft and into their new wooden monastery on December 7, 1944.

It had been a tough but successful first year. The monks had put in crops of wheat, corn and cotton, and planted a vegetable garden. Applications came in steadily, and postulants from across the country were

LEFT: *Conyers under construction, and an aerial view of the monastery today.*

soon filling up the small dormitory. There was rarely a lull between building projects at Holy Ghost.

In May of 1946, the first General Chapter since the start of World War II convened at Citeaux. At the end of that session, Holy Ghost was elevated to abbey status. But first there was some debate over the correctness of Dom Frederic's decision to move ahead on the Conyers deal without getting official permission from the order first. Ultimately, it was agreed that, under the extraordinary circumstances of war, the consent of the Apostolic Delegate was enough to satisfy the requirement. A month later, on June 6, Father James Fox was elected the first abbot of Holy Ghost Abbey. On October 18, he received his abbatial blessing.

No sooner than Gethsemani's first daughterhouse was up and running, a second one was in the works. This time Dom Frederic looked to the West. He chose a site near Salt Lake City, Utah: 1,800 acres in an isolated valley high in the Ogden Canyon. Though the Utah landscape was forbidding in its stark contrasts of snow-capped peak and river basin, the land offered rich soil and an environment that seemed to echo the Cistercian ideals of silence and seclusion.

The William Parke Farm, as it was known, cost Dom Frederic $100,000. He bought it on March 4, 1947. There were no buildings on that land, but the abbot refused to let that stand in the way of his plans to launch a foundation in June. He hired a local contractor to build a monastery out of metal Quonset huts, a quick and cheap way to solve the problem, he believed. But there were delays in securing the huts, and soon it was clear to Dom Frederic that he had to consider other ways to house his men in the interim. This time, he bought used Army barracks and arranged for them to be transported to the farm. Again he relied on local con-

OPPOSITE TOP: *Dom Frederic, behind the cross at left, and the other founders of Holy Trinity, leaving for Utah.*
OPPOSITE BOTTOM: *Dormitory cells at Holy Trinity.*
TOP LEFT: *"Temporary" Quonset hut design that still stands today.*
ABOVE: *Sketch of original plans for the monastery and church, never carried out.*

143

tractors, who said they could set up the barracks quickly so his men would have a place to sleep when they arrived.

On July 7, Dom Frederic sent 34 of his more than 170 monks to Utah. They left Gethsemani in the evening, carrying their replica of the founding cross, and arrived at their new home three days later. A chartered bus drove them up the winding canyon to the farm, where not only had the huts not arrived, but neither had all the barracks. But the next day something far more amazing than a Quonset-hut monastery found its way to the farm. The colony received its first postulant, a man on a bicycle who had heard that Trappists were coming to the Ogden Valley and wanted to join the community.

During their first months in Utah, the founders of what would become the Abbey of Our Lady of the Holy Trinity spent most of their time and energy constructing a home. The barracks, which had once been home to German and Italian war prisoners, gave the monks a place to sleep until the "temporary" Quonset-hut monastery was completed the following year. As it turned out, that odd steel structure with its industrial-warehouse appearance was never replaced with anything "permanent." Today it is still home to the monks of Holy Trinity, and there are no plans to replace it.

The monastery's non-traditional look and out-of-the-way location didn't keep men from sending their applications to Holy Trinity. By January of 1948, the community had attracted more postulants, swelling their number to 41. Today there are 24 monks at Holy Trinity and a farm devoted to crops of alfalfa, barley and hay, as well as grazing land for beef cattle.

THE 100TH ANNIVERSARY OF THE FOUNDING OF Gethsemani was approaching, and Dom Frederic began planning for it. But it was a busy year, from the start, and he was on the road a great deal throughout the spring and summer.

THE SPECIAL RELATIONSHIP BETWEEN GETHSEMANI AND ST. THÉRÈSE OF LISIEUX GREW OUT OF A DECISION DOM FREDERIC MADE WHILE HE WAS PRIOR. DURING ONE OF DOM EDMOND'S ABSENCES, HE SELECTED THÉRÈSE'S AUTOBIOGRAPHY, "THE STORY OF A SOUL," AS THE DAILY READING IN THE REFECTORY. THE SIMPLE SPIRITUALITY OF THE FRENCH NUN WHO DIED OF TUBERCULOSIS AT 24 HAD A PROFOUND EFFECT ON THE MONKS.

IT WAS DOM EDMOND, HOWEVER, WHO CEMENTED THE TRANS-CONTINENTAL BOND BETWEEN THE ABBEY AND THÉRÈSE'S THREE SISTERS. IN 1926, HE PERSONALLY VISITED THE LISIEUX CONVENT WHERE THÉRÈSE DIED IN 1897 AND LATER BEGAN A CORRESPONDENCE WITH HER SISTERS. IN EACH LETTER, HE ENCLOSED A DONATION TO HER SHRINE.

EVENTUALLY HER SISTERS AT LISIEUX DECIDED TO "ADOPT" HIM AS THEIR BROTHER. TO INDICATE THÉRÈSE'S AGREEMENT, THEY CUT OUT THE WORD "MOI" FROM HER WRITINGS AND ATTACHED IT TO THE "ACT OF ADOPTION."

Gethsemani's third foundation, Mepkin Abbey in South Carolina.

He was home again in July, anticipating the harvests to come – from Gethsemani's fields and Fr. Louis' book.

Then August arrived and, ignoring his long history of poor health and the mounting evidence that his heart was failing, Dom Frederic set out by train for Georgia to make his visitation. In an empty compartment of that train, in the predawn hours of August 4, after calling for help, Dom Frederic suffered a final, fatal heart attack. A porter heard his cries and tried to help as the train pulled into the Knoxville station, but his efforts came too late.

In a notebook discovered some 40 years later, Fr. Louis described in detail Dom Frederic's last words to the community, spoken in the chapter room the morning he left for Georgia. The 74-year-old abbot took that moment to urge his monks not just to tolerate each other's differences but to welcome them as gifts from God. His last lesson was "typical," in Fr. Louis' words – "forceful, fervent, austere, uncompromising, yet tempered by gentleness and sympathy."

The monks of Gethsemani learned of their abbot's death by telephone an hour after it was discovered. In a letter he wrote later that day, Fr. Louis shared the sad news with a friend, putting into words what many others, inside and outside the monastery, felt about Dom Frederic.

In March, he met with Henry and Clare Boothe Luce in South Carolina to talk about their desire to give Gethsemani their Mepkin Plantation, a 7,000-acre estate near Charleston.

May was spent in Utah, visiting the foundation and at home, recovering from a car accident. In June, he traveled to Rhode Island to visit Our Lady of the Valley, which had recently been raised to the status of an abbey.

"I suddenly realized how much I owed to this abbot who was in every sense a Father to us . . . ," Fr. Louis wrote. "Say a prayer for him, although I don't think he needs too much help."

GETHSEMANI CONTINUES to GROW

1936: Phone system is installed. Electric lights replace gas lamps in entire monastery, including church. Monks' cemetery expands south.

1937: New water tank is in operation. Retreat house is refurbished; now has 42 renovated rooms. More than 3,000 bushels of wheat, barley and oats and 4,000 pounds of corn are harvested.

1938: Dom Frederic's Lake opens. Sheet-metal roofing is applied to infirmary, and novitiate roof is replaced with tar paper. Annex is built to cow barn for calving.

1940: Retaining wall and novitiate annex (chapel) are finished. Excavation for new kitchen begins on cloister's east wing.

1941: Excavation under chapter room begins. Area will contain lavatories and showers for professed and novice brothers when complete.

1944: New garage is built on site of old chicken coop and dovecote.

1947: Horse barn is finished.

OPPOSITE LEFT: Dom Frederic at the lake that bears his name. LEFT: The monastery's growing farm. ABOVE: Farm buildings under construction. BELOW: Monks building the novitiate and the dam at Dom Frederic's Lake.

Monks working on new Bldg (not guest bldg.)

DOM JAMES FOX:
FROM HARVARD to HERMITAGE
1948-1967

Within a year of his election as the sixth abbot of Gethsemani, Dom James Fox authorized the publication of a book celebrating the abbey's 100th anniversary. It was called *Gethsemani Magnificat,* an elegant title that underscored the abbey's devotion to Mary and its bonds to Medieval Europe.

And yet, there was nothing elegant or European about the book's message. It was a virile, intensely patriotic, almost militant image of monasticism that Dom James projected to readers of *Gethsemani Magnificat.* In his rousing introduction, he left no doubt that once again times were changing at the oldest Trappist abbey in America.

"The acid test of any dynasty, nation or institution is time," Dom James began. Clearly Gethsemani had passed that test with flying colors. The house now bulged at its seams with 165 monks, while its two foundations in Georgia and Utah lodged 110 more men between them. The question that Dom James posed next was nothing if not rhetorical: "Could red-blooded American boys, accustomed as they are to freedom, action and independence, ever measure up to the high heroic requirements of the Trappist ideal?"

Many of Gethsemani's 70 novices that year were World War II veterans, young men who had served in the Army, paratroopers, Navy and Marines. Now they were living a different kind of life, but they were still heroes in Dom James' mind, defending "their beloved Homeland and American way of life." This time, however, their battles were fought not on the beaches of Europe or in the air over Japan but in the trenches of Trappist life. Gethsemani and its daughterhouses, its abbot predicted, would become "powerhouses of prayer and penance," serving the nation as its "prime bulwarks of defense against the rising tides of atheism and terrorism." There was a fiery optimism in the tone of his final paragraph, which matched the "can do" attitude of America in those days

Top: *Installation and blessing of the new church bells.*
Above: *A pottery cup, used by the monks of Gethsemani.*

leading up to the long Cold War: "At Gethsemani, boys give – not fifty percent, seventy percent, ninety percent, nor even ninety-five percent – but one hundred percent for God and country."

Gethsemani Magnificat came out in April of 1949, an extraordinarily hopeful time in the history of America and much of the world. NATO was born that spring, as was the Republic of Eire. It was the year that Radio Free Europe penetrated the Iron Curtain and the British stopped rationing clothing. The hit Broadway musical *South Pacific* featured a song called "A Cockeyed Optimist."

Gethsemani's abbot was hopeful, too. And rightly so. Before the year was out, he would dispatch another two dozen monks to South Carolina to make a third foundation, and two years later a fourth colony would found a house in upstate New York. Yet even with all those men gone, Dom James found himself confronting a most perplexing problem in 1952: how to make room for 275 men in a monastery built to house 70.

Gethsemani's acid test, as it turned out, would not be time but space.

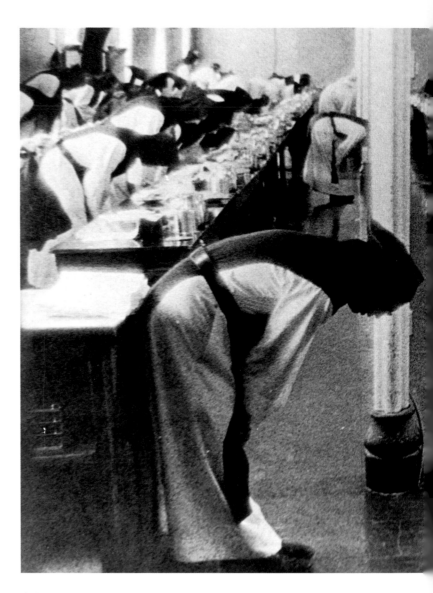

To THOSE WHO KNOW GETHSEMANI PRIMARILY through the works of Thomas Merton, particularly through his private journals, Dom James is often reduced to a one-dimensional character with a single purpose in life: to be the thorn in the author's side. Casual readers often misinterpret the complicated and respectful relationship between the two monks (Dom James chose Fr. Louis as his personal confessor, after all), and dismiss as rigid and tyrannical an abbot who was in fact a complex individual and innovative administrator. In the process, they oversimplify both men.

Throughout his years at Gethsemani, Fr. Louis struggled to integrate his life as a writer with his life as a contemplative, and to balance his responsibilities to his community with his desire for greater solitude. More often than not, in his diaries, he couched those internal debates with himself in terms of external conflicts with Dom James. In his private musings, particularly in the 1960s, Fr. Louis tended to portray the abbot as his nemesis: a narrow-minded dictator determined to thwart his every hope and aspiration for 20 long years.

In truth Dom James had a personal style and monastic career every bit as ambivalent and contradictory as that of Fr. Louis. As abbot of Gethsemani for two of its most dynamic decades, Dom James was both progressive and cautious. Like Fr. Louis, he was unpredictable and inconsistent, vexing traits for those who like to classify leaders into neat categories.

Dom James was a trailblazer in some arenas. He revamped the process by which applicants to the

monastery were selected, adding psychological evaluations to the equation. He supported reforms that ultimately changed his monks' clothing, broadened their ability to change residence from one monastery to another, and enhanced their chances for living a hermit's life.

Today, some who knew him as abbot describe Dom James as a gracious and generous monk whose spiritual side was most remarkable for its childlike innocence. While his reputation was that of an efficient and businesslike administrator, he was also known for a religious sensibility that bordered on the naive and sentimental.

His favorite saying, which he had imprinted on a rubber stamp, was "All for Jesus, through Mary, with a smile." Indeed, those exact words were tacked on, like an Amen, to the end of his otherwise tough-talking introduction to *Gethsemani Magnificat*.

He is remembered by some as a formidable opponent in a debate and a headstrong leader. There is little disagreement about his business sense. He was a shrewd administrator whose work experience, before coming to the abbey, gave him valuable insight into the finer points of corporate finance. (He could be a good manager of people, too. Former Br. Clement, Gethsemani's cellarer for 15 years before leaving the monastery, said of Dom James: "He was very good at knowing intuitively each one of his men.") His *magna cum laude* degree and his studies at the Harvard School of Business Administration certainly preceded him wherever he went, both inside and outside the monastery. Such a distinguished educational background provided an easy stereotype for those who didn't know the abbot well.

But his legendary Harvard degree, like Fr. Louis' occasional depiction of him as a despot in his diaries, does not tell the whole story of Dom James.

A few facts: He was born in 1896, about the time Gethsemani was reeling from its college scandal. He grew up in Dedham, Massachusetts, not far from Boston. This geographical fact of his life would come back to haunt Dom James: years later in his obituary, The Louisville *Courier-Journal* would mistakenly identify him as a native of Boston, Kentucky, a town several miles northwest of the monastery.

Dom James joined the Navy Reserves in February 1918 and was commissioned as ensign on the *U.S.S. Aroostook* that spring. For the next year, he performed finance-related jobs at several Navy offices in Massachusetts. In June 1919, he resigned from active duty and went to work for the U.S. Treasury Department as a

ABOVE: *Dom James Fox.* OPPOSITE: *Novices taking part in a traditional Corpus Christi procession in the cloister, which is carpeted in flower petals.*

revenue agent in the income tax division. His job was to inspect the tax returns of corporations.

"This gave me a vivid opportunity to study men in the grand pursuit of making money and of scaling the heights to fame and fortune," Dom James wrote to his Harvard classmates at the time of his 25th reunion in 1943. "But instead of becoming hypnotized also and drawn into the grand whirlpool, I reacted diametrically opposite. I found myself asking myself, is this what life is for, to burn it up in sweating, steaming, and toiling in a race for power, prestige, passion, pleasure and piles of stocks and bonds, from every one of which I am going to be separated some day?"

His answer was a resounding "No." In 1927 he rejected once and for all the "grand whirlpool" and entered Gethsemani.

He was serving as guestmaster in 1941 when Fr. Louis' brother, John Paul Merton, a sergeant in the Royal Canadian Air Force, stopped by the monastery for a visit while on leave. Though he did not know the guestmaster well at the time, Fr. Louis arranged for him to prepare John Paul for his baptism into the Catholic faith. This was the first of many emotional bonds that would connect the two monks.

A few years later, Dom James left Gethsemani when he was chosen to become superior of the founding group in Georgia. In 1946, that community – originally known as the Abbey of the Holy Ghost but later changed to Holy Spirit – elected him abbot, a job he held until he was called back to Kentucky to serve as a witness to the election of Dom Frederic's successor.

Dom Bernard Johnson, the current abbot of the Abbey of the Holy Spirit, remembers the community's reaction when Dom James left. "He won't be back," some predicted. In a sense, they were right. At Gethsemani, he was elected to succeed Dom Frederic. And though Dom James was to return to Conyers many times after that, it would be for visitations only, in his new role as Father Immediate of the Georgia house.

In a diary that was later published as *The Sign of Jonas,* Fr. Louis described his first impression of the new abbot, one that would change dramatically over time. In August 1948, a few days after the election, Fr. Louis wrote: "Dom James is quiet and humble." In May of the following year, in a passage about their mutual desire for greater solitude and their shared attraction to the hermit life, Fr. Louis refers to his abbot as "such a saint." Somewhere between humble sainthood and absolute dictatorship lies the true character of Dom James Fox.

THE YEAR 1949 BEGAN AT GETHSEMANI WITH influenza and ended with a new foundation. In between, a series of historic events played themselves out. The first Trappistines in the U.S., a group of Irish and American women, settled at Wrentham, Massachusetts. At least one Gethsemani Chapter talk, a time traditionally set aside for consideration of monastic topics, focused on the growing threat of atomic warfare. The Rhode Island monastery at Our Lady of the Valley,

SECTION 1   THE COURIER-JOURNAL, LOUISVILLE, KY.

Thousands Share Gethsemani Peace

Trappists Mark Full Century For Monastery

By DON FREEMAN
Courier-Journal Staff Writer.

Trappist, Ky., June 1—Thousands of people from many parts of a harassed world were here today to share the holy peacefulness of Our Lady of Gethsemani Monastery.

Officially they attended to help this austere Trappist institution celebrate its 100th anniversary.

But more than that, "you were drawn by that instinct which tells you God is in this place," the Rt. Rev. Dom M. James Fox, abbot of Gethsemani, told the throng.

People Stand In Hot Sun.

People flocked here as early as dawn, although the vivid processions opening the celebration did not start until 9:30.

During the outdoor solemn pontifical Mass, they stood in the hot sun when they were not kneeling.

Afterward they sauntered across the grounds, absorbing the spirit of the medieval stone buildings, the silver spire of the monastery basilica, the statue of Joseph and the infant Jesus crowning the hill near by, and the quiet fields.

As the basilica bell tolled at 9:30, the Most Rev. John A. Floersh, archbishop of Louisville, was escorted directly from the monastery to the outdoor altar.

There he kneeled while another procession of church dignitaries, numbering about 500 with their attendants, moved toward the altar by a longer route.

In this procession, his long red train held by a monk, was Dennis Cardinal Dougherty, archbishop of Philadelphia. His red vestments were trimmed in ermine. The 83-year-old cardinal had attended both the 50th and the 75th anniversaries of the monastery.

Marching ahead of him were the abbot general of the Trappist order, the Rt. Rev. Dom M. Dominic Nogues, from Rome and the mother house at Citeaux, France; Archbishop Yu Pin of China; 12 bishops, and 11 abbots of various orders.

Clements, Chapman Look On.

Marching, too, were the members of the monastery. Many were husky and youthful. And then there was the old, stooped one who sweated as he tapped his cane along the gravel path.

There were Trappist monks from other monasteries in the United States, from Canada, and from China. There were white-robed Dominicans, Franciscans in brown or black, Passionists in

Courier-Journal Photos by Cort Best.

COLORFUL PROCESSIONS opened ceremonies marking the 100th anniversary of Our Lady of Gethsemani Monastery. A cardinal, two archbishops, 12 bishops, and 11 abbots were among the marchers from the monastery to the outdoor altar for a Mass.

which had become an abbey in 1946, burned to the ground in a tragic fire on March 21, 1950.

And on June 1, a day so bright that it sunburned the necks of Gethsemani's monks, the abbey's long-anticipated centennial celebration went off without a hitch. Monsignor Fulton J. Sheen delivered an enthusiastic speech into several microphones set up for the occasion. His booming voice, praising the Trappist life, stirred the crowd that had gathered in a field outside the enclosure. Television cam-

ABOVE: *News coverage of the centennial, with photos of Dom James and Louisville Archbishop John Floersh.*

TOP RIGHT: *Cistercian Abbot General Dominique Nogues and Monsignor Fulton J. Sheen confer during celebration.*

OPPOSITE: *The makeshift dormitory built in the preau and novices seeking solitude in an over-crowded monastery.*

BOTTOM: *Gethsemani at its peak population.*

eras from WHAS in Louisville and newsreel crews from Fox Movietone recorded the event.

The following year, war erupted in Korea when Communist troops from the North invaded the South, capturing the city of Seoul. The United Nations intervened, sending its forces into the battle. While the world watched this volatile situation, Gethsemani was quietly coping with yet another avalanche of letters from men wanting to try Trappist life.

But the monastery did not have enough room for the 270 men already living there. By 1951, the threat of fire breaking out or floors falling in was real. Dom James resolved the crisis – at least temporarily – with a dose of Yankee ingenuity. First his monks built a framework structure inside the cloister courtyard customarily reserved for quiet reading and meditation. They then covered the structure with a huge tarpaulin, boarded up the sides and floor beneath the tent and added straw mattresses – creating, in effect, a makeshift dormitory.

It was a drastic measure designed to deal with a desperate situation. Fifty monks lived there for two years. Many still tell stories about their boots freezing to the floorboards overnight during the bitterly cold winter months. Meanwhile, the dormitory where the choir monks slept was crammed with extra sleeping stalls, known as cells. They were jammed along the walls in whatever space could be found between windows.

Gethsemani needed more room: it was that simple. Soon the racket of jackhammers and cement mixers drowned out the more familiar Nelson County sounds of songbirds and distant trains. In 1952, on a hill across the state road that bisects the monastery property, a yellow brick "family guest house" was completed and immediately put to use. Work was also underway on an 80-room retreat house. Br. Giles Naughton, the architect who had studied at Catholic University, designed both these projects in a style strongly influenced by Frank Lloyd Wright. In 1960, a small one-story motel was built across from the family guesthouse to accommodate additional visitors.

Other innovations came about: a series of monk-made lakes; fluorescent reading lights in the choir stalls; additional church bells; a water-treatment plant.

THE OLD GETHSEMANI WAS GIVING WAY TO the new, and not only in terms of bricks and mortar.

Dom James revitalized the intellectual and liturgical life at Gethsemani as well. Twice, at his invitation, Professor Francois Lefevre, a French authority on Gregorian chant, led a series of intensive classes at Gethsemani to improve the quality of the community's choral prayer. Following his visits, two European Benedictine music scholars – Dom Ludovic Baron and Dom Jean Desroquettes – helped to hone Gethsemani's chant skills over a period of years. When Fr. Chrysogonus Waddell joined the community in 1950, the monastery's music program received yet another boost. Professionally trained at the Philadelphia Conservatory of Music, Fr. Chrysogonus became choirmaster in the late 1950s and, at the time of the shift from Latin to English, created a new plainchant comparable to Gregorian, which is sung

ABOVE: *A monk at work.* LEFT: *The family guest house.* BELOW: *The new retreat house.* OPPOSITE: *The gazebo in the preau.*

not only at Gethsemani but at other monastic communities and parishes.

In 1951, the selection of Fr. Louis as master of scholastics signaled Dom James' desire to elevate the standards of monastic training at Gethsemani. Drawing on lessons learned at Cambridge and Columbia University as well as his religious training, Fr. Louis revived and expanded the curriculum. Out of his classes came the monastery's next generation of thinkers and leaders.

In 1960, in an effort to further improve the quality of instruction for monks studying to be priests, Dom James invited New York philosophy professor Dan Walsh, an old friend of Merton from his Columbia University days, to come to Gethsemani to teach. Walsh stayed on for many years, dividing his time between the abbey and a visiting professorship at Bellarmine College in Louisville.

Walsh had been instrumental in Merton's decision to become a Trappist and was also the mutual friend who introduced Merton and Tommie O'Callaghan, Walsh's former student from his days as a professor at New York's Manhattanville College of the Sacred Heart. Through Walsh, Mrs. O'Callaghan and her husband, Frank, became close friends of Merton, who often visited their home when he was in Louisville on business. Mrs. O'Callaghan later was a founding trustee of the Thomas Merton Legacy Trust.

Walsh lived at Gethsemani off and on for several years before his ordination as a priest on May 14, 1967, and at his death was buried in the abbey cemetery. His philosophy classes and his impromptu sessions held on the front lawn of the monastery are still remembered fondly by those in the community who participated in them.

159

THE OLD ADAGE ABOUT THE RIGHT ABBOT COMING ALONG at the right time was demonstrating itself once again. Faced with a post-war mandate from his Trappist superiors to make Gethsemani a self-sufficient house, Dom James must surely have fallen back on his experience working for the Treasury Department. It was obvious that Gethsemani could not subsist on the meager income derived from its farm operation or its local sales of dairy, bakery and meat products. Perhaps he could draw from what he had learned while studying corporate financial records as a young tax inspector.

Dom James took a bold step. He established Gethsemani Farms as the business arm of the monastery and charged it with producing, packaging and marketing all the abbey's food products, including a new item that would soon be available – fruitcake.

John Dorsey, a civil engineer, and Brother Frederic Collins, who had a degree in business administration as well as experience working for Ford Motor Company, developed the business.

TOP: *The gatehouse store.*
RIGHT: *Brother Raphael Prendergast surveying monastery land.*

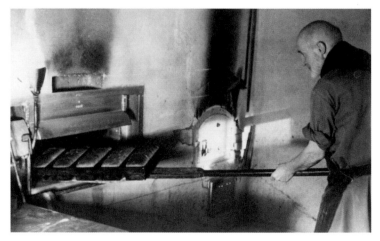

Joining them in 1957 was Brother Raphael Prendergast, who came to the monastery after years in the construction business. Both Br. Frederic, who is now treasurer of Gethsemani, and Br. Raphael, who is prior, were World War II veterans. Under their supervision, Gethsemani Farms became a thriving mail-order food business, and the monastery became completely self-supporting.

In 1953, a fire destroyed the old cow barn. A new cow barn was built across the road in a field near the new family guest house. On the old site, using the hefty stone walls of the barn as a framework, the monks eventually built a new structure, called the Farms Building, to house the cheese-packaging operation and provide storage. A wing was later added so fruitcakes could be made in the same building. Electric fans made their debut in the mid-1950s.

During this period of intense growth at home, Gethsemani was also expanding the borders of Trappist influence into other states. Our Lady of Mepkin was founded on November 14, 1949, in Moncks Corner, South Carolina, on a plantation donated by Henry and Clare Boothe Luce. It became an abbey in 1955.

In 1951, a colony of Gethsemani monks founded Our Lady of Genesee monastery in upstate New York. In 1955, a fifth foundation, Our Lady of New Clairvaux, was made in northern California at Vina.

The sixth and final daughterhouse was established in Chile in 1966, near the end of the 20-year regime of Dom James. Prior to making this foundation, the abbot and his cellarer had visited Bergen, Norway, at the invitation of the bishop who wanted a Trappist monastery in his diocese. When those plans didn't work out, the door was open for Gethsemani to take over the Chilean monastery. That house was originally a foundation of the Trappists at Spencer, Massachusetts, who also had a

house in Argentina. When they decided two South American monasteries were too much to handle, Gethsemani stepped in and assumed responsibility for the one in Chile.

Originally situated on property close to Santiago, the monastery of Miraflores moved 80 miles south of the city as urban sprawl came too close for comfort for its monks. They relocated on land where they now raise cattle and grow almonds and pistachio nuts. The community, which numbers about 25 today, is mostly made up of Latin American monks. They are using the profits they earn from the sale and development of their Santiago property to support housing programs for Chile's poor.

THROUGHOUT THE 1950S, THE SPECTER OF FLAME stalked Dom James. He was well aware of the history of destructive fires at Trappist monasteries in America. What's more, Gethsemani had witnessed some awesome blazes of its own. In the mid-'50s, both a cow barn and a grain barn burned, and more than once small fires were discovered – and doused – in various buildings outside

the enclosure and in the woods. Particularly at a time of overcrowding, fire was a real and present danger.

Not long after Our Lady of the Valley went down in flames in Rhode Island, Dom James instituted a nightly fire watch at Gethsemani. Under this system, a monk made the rounds of the monastery at day's end, punching a clock to verify his inspection. In *The Sign of Jonas,* Fr. Louis wrote eloquently of his own experiences on the fire watch in July 1952. By 1956, the abbot had purchased a fire engine, initiated a firefighting program and built a fire tower.

That still wasn't enough to ease his mind. In the late 1950s, Dom James decided to fireproof the monastery and, in the process, renovate the deteriorating buildings that housed his men. Architect William Schickel, of Loveland, Ohio, was invited to design the renovation of the church, cloister and cloister courtyard, or *preau.* Maurice Lavanoux, editor of *Liturgical Arts,* had urged Dom James to consider Schickel, based on the success of his Grailville Oratory.

Schickel's plan was to remove the interior Gothic shell of the century-old church and, in the process,

ABOVE: *Motivated by fires like this one at the sheep barn, Dom James instituted a nightly fire watch.* LEFT: *The clock that monks punched to verify each fire-watch inspection.* OPPOSITE: *Founders of the daughterhouse at Vina, California, en route from the Gethsemani train station, and monks at Genesee, New York.*

expose the stark structures beneath it. He believed the church's massive Old World ornamentation and its dark stained-glass windows bore no organic relationship to the materials the monks had used to build it, nor to its rural Kentucky setting. Schickel wanted to strip away the plaster and lath arches and the fake vaulting to reveal the simplicity of the church's bare brick walls. He advocated replacing the deeply hued Munich windows with pale modern glass in patterns of abstract geometric design to allow more light into the church. When the

project was completed, the brick walls were covered in white paint and the timber roof beams were permanently exposed.

The cloister and *preau* were renovated in similar fashion, in a 1950s architectural style known as "Brutalist." What had been a grassy courtyard divided into four sections by a pattern of foot paths was made into something far less comforting or bucolic. Writing in *Liturgical Arts* at the time, Father Matthew Kelty described the renovated *preau* as "strangely urban," and said it reminded him of being "back in Detroit or down-

Top: *Views of the church before and after major renovation.*
Right: *A view during the renovation.*
Opposite: *A view of the preau after it was renovated in the "Brutalist" style, and a monk walking down the redesigned cloister.*

town Boston." Certainly the street lamps placed at the four corners of the square contributed to Fr. Matthew's vision of the revamped space as an inner-city courtyard.

Schickel's renovations reflected liturgical reforms taking place contemporaneously in the church. The bywords of his redesign were "light, clarity and simplicity"– basic elements of classic Cistercian spirituality, but also terms that were gaining cachet as the spirit of the Second Vatican Council began to act upon the broader Catholic consciousness.

Spiritually and physically, the chaos of this massive renovation project was hard on the monks who lived in the midst of it. It's impossible not to see this time of tearing down and rebuilding as a metaphor for what was happening within the Catholic Church itself at the time. On a literal level, the monks of Gethsemani were ripping apart all that had taken their forebears a century to create. On a figurative level, all of this mirrored the agonizing process of institutional reform and rebirth triggered by Vatican II.

"It was a terrific symbol," Br. Raphael says today. "The place looked like London in the blitz. It was diffi-

cult to live with – the jackhammers, air compressors, power saws, the workmen hollering through those years. But something new was coming."

That something new was as demanding and rigorous as anything any Trappist had endured in the past. But the community survived. It withstood the massive rearrangement of everything familiar, the disruption of all routine, the deprivation of sleep, the impossibility of solitude and, most disturbing of all, the loss of silence. Living through a renovation, as any homeowner who has done it can testify, is a painful process for even the most active members of society. It is not what one imagines as a backdrop for contemplative prayer.

Fr. Matthew, in his magazine piece, frankly expressed surprise that Dom James had successfully pulled off such a risky enterprise. He lived through it and still could not explain how it was accomplished.

When you consider the general conservatism of the Church, of religious orders, the monastic in particular, and of the contemplative variety perhaps more than others, and of Gethsemani in this instance, it is perhaps something of an understatement to say all this was an achievement.

AND THE RENOVATIONS OF THE MONASTERY WERE JUST the tip of the iceberg. Vatican II also ushered in reforms that led to sweeping changes in the Cistercian Order. Rituals and rules that Trappists had lived by for nearly nine centuries were phased out.

In 1948, the year Dom James was elected, it was something of a shock when monks were allowed to shave themselves. Weekly shears had long been the custom – lay brothers trimmed in one group, choir monks in another. But by 1965, significant changes had transformed just about every arena of monastic life – including what kind of clothes a monk wore, when he prayed, what he ate, where he could walk, to whom he could speak. Indeed, the very fact that he could talk at all would have been inconceivable a few years earlier.

In the midst of such change, one of the oldest elements of Cistercian life was eliminated: the lay brothers, or *conversi,* as they are also called. Cistercians certainly didn't invent lay brothers; they existed before the Order did. But from the time of Citeaux, the lay brothers played an important role in Cistercian life.

In the Middle Ages, they were primarily skilled workers from the uneducated class who would not have met the standards required of choir monks. They performed the manual labor at monasteries and, over the centuries, helped develop a unique spirituality, attuned

The hermitage where Dom James lived after his resignation as abbot in 1967.

to nature and everyday tasks. Writing in his diaries in the mid-1960s, Fr. Louis went so far as to suggest the lay brother vocation was "more authentic" than that of the choir monk.

In modern times, particularly since World War II, many who entered the lay brother novitiate were middle-class and college-educated, often men with professional work experience like Br. Frederic and Br. Raphael. Increasingly they held positions in their monasteries that were once reserved for choir monks. In the 1950s, for example, John Dorsey became the first lay brother to serve as cellarer at Gethsemani.

After Vatican II, however, a series of votes were taken by The General Chapter which led to the merger of lay brothers and choir monks into one class of Cistercians. In effect, it was less of a merger than a submersion, as some have called it. What happened was that the lay brothers became choir monks. They adopted the choir monk's clothing, rituals and prayer routines, all of which were quite different from those of their own distinct tradition.

There would no longer be training in that tradition. All monks were to be part of a common novitiate, sharing the same rights and duties – with one exception. Only priests would be allowed to fill the positions of abbot, prior and novice master. But even that distinction has been modified over the years; Brother Gerlac O'Loughlin and Br. Raphael, for example, were the first

tain their way of life. At Gethsemani, a few have acted on that option. A small group still prays separately – saying the traditional lay-brother office of "Aves" and "Paters" in a quiet room – while the rest of the community gathers in the choir to sing and chant six times a day.

DOM JAMES WAS ABBOT FOR 20 YEARS WHEN HE MADE it known in the fall of 1967 that he wished to resign and become a hermit. His legacy is a rich and varied one. When he headed for his hermitage on the hill, Dom James left a community 125-monks strong with daughterhouses from coast to coast, as well as one in South America. The face and the reputation of Gethsemani had changed forever. Thanks in large part to his fellow hermit and perennial sparring partner, Merton, Gethsemani in 1968 was arguably the best-known Trappist monastery in the world.

Dom James lived out his final years in a hermitage designed and built for him by his cellarer of 15 years. It was Dorsey's last project before leaving the monastery in 1969. " You could see for miles around," Dorsey recalls. "There was no water, and no way to get water." He had to blast a hole in the hill to make a foundation. Then he used the rock from that hillside to build two of the hermitage walls. Most of the rest was glass to take advantage of the view.

Dom James' life as a hermit came to an abrupt end on April 16, 1977. On that Saturday, two men from nearby New Hope, Kentucky, broke into the hermitage and severely beat Dom James. He was found the next morning by Brother Norbert Meier who drove up in a Jeep to take Dom James to Sunday Mass. His attackers were later apprehended, convicted and sent to prison.

Too feeble to live alone after the attack, Dom James eventually moved into the new infirmary, where he died on Good Friday, 1987, at the age of 91. His hermitage still stands today, an out-of-the-way monument to the sixth abbot of Gethsemani.

two priors of Gethsemani to come from outside the ranks of its priests.

Some Trappists today feel the unification decree did away with a vital Cistercian vocation. They believe there is room for the lay-brother branch of monasticism which emphasizes manual labor and private prayer, and complements the choir monk's life, which is characterized by more intense study and more frequent periods of common prayer.

Under the original unification resolution, those who were already professed as *conversi* were allowed to main-

GETHSEMANI:
A WORK in PROGRESS

1949: Gethsemani makes third foundation, Our Lady of Mepkin, in South Carolina.

1950: Gethsemani church is consecrated as a basilica.

1951: More than 270 men live at Gethsemani, at least 50 of them sleeping in a makeshift dormitory in the cloister courtyard; a fourth foundation, Our Lady of Genesee, is made in upstate New York; Dom James establishes Gethsemani Farms, the business that produces and sells cheese, meat and fruitcakes.

1953: Cow barn burns, and the site eventually becomes Farms Building.

1955: A fifth foundation, Our Lady of New Clairvaux, is made at Vina, California.

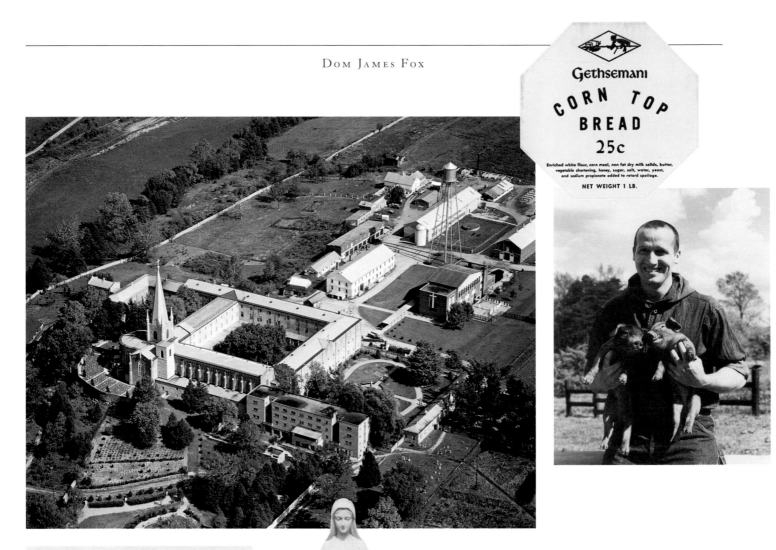

Gethsemani
CORN TOP
BREAD
25c

Enriched white flour, corn meal, non fat dry milk solids, butter,
vegetable shortening, honey, sugar, salt, water, yeast,
and sodium propionate added to retard spoilage.

NET WEIGHT 1 LB.

1956: Fire tower goes up; Gethsemani acquires the Linton Farm and Hannekamp's Holler.

1960: Monks plant 200 acres of alfalfa for livestock feed and raise Duroc hogs for smoked-ham business.

1962: Architect William Schickel is hired to renovate the church and cloister.

1966: Gethsemani has 150 members, making it the largest Cistercian community in the world; Gethsemani takes over foundation in Chile.

1967: Renovation and fireproofing are completed.

169

FATHER FLAVIAN BURNS:
QUIETING DOWN
1968-1973

L. M. Flavian Burns, ocso.

A TRADITIONAL "VOTING" VESSEL, USED IN TRAPPIST ELECTIONS. EACH PROFESSED MONK RECEIVES THREE SMALL BALLS OR MARBLES WITH WHICH TO CAST HIS BALLOT. THE MARBLES ARE OF DIFFERENT COLORS, INDICATING A VOTE IN FAVOR, IN OPPOSITION OR IN ABSTENTION. TWO MONKS SIT ON EITHER SIDE OF THE VOTING VESSEL TO COLLECT THE UNUSED MARBLES. WHEN ALL HAVE VOTED, THE ABBOT COUNTS THE BALLOTS, TURNS THE URN UPSIDE DOWN TO SHOW IT IS EMPTY AND ANNOUNCES THE RESULTS OF THE VOTE.

ARLY IN JANUARY OF 1968, U.S. MILITARY involvement in Vietnam was escalating, as was the anti-war movement back home. The Tet Offensive was only weeks away. Deep divisions over race, politics and generational values were also surfacing on campuses and in the streets as the new year began. By spring, this volatile cultural climate would erupt into violence, and by summer, Americans would be struggling, one against the other, in the wake of widespread grief and unrest. It was a year not soon to be forgotten.

In the midst of this turmoil, or rather on the margins of it, Father Flavian Burns was living as a hermit, alone in a cabin tucked in the woods, a mile or so out from the abbey. In 1966, with the blessing of Dom James, Fr. Flavian had moved to this hermitage, a one-story cottage built over the course of a summer with the help of Brothers Ralph and Alfred. They used scrap material salvaged from other building projects, including discarded shutters and windows from the newly renovated monastery. Detached not only from the chaos of the outside world but even from the daily life of his own monastery, Fr. Flavian was content with his rather aloof role in the community when, at the close of 1967, Dom James let it be known he wished to resign. The abbot who had led Gethsemani through two decades of bustling growth was now 71 years old.

Whom would the community elect to replace him?

Despite Fr. Flavian's avowed desire to lead a life of solitude in the woods, the community elected him to succeed Dom James. The tall, soft-spoken monk with the New Jersey accent found himself at a vocational crossroads that would become familiar territory to him over the next three decades. His quest for a simpler life with emphasis on contemplative ideals was being challenged by the call to assume a more active leadership role within the community and (by virtue of being abbot of Gethsemani) within the Cistercian Order internationally. Fr. Flavian would find this to be a pattern in his life

The hermitage where Father Flavian lived
before and after his abbacy.

as a Trappist – the cycling back and forth from hermitage to abbot's office. Over the next 30 years, he would serve not only as abbot of Gethsemani from 1968 to 1973, but eventually hold the titles of temporary superior and abbot at two other Trappist monasteries, always interspersing these periods of activity with time living alone.

Though at the time of his first election as abbot he had served in several positions of authority within the community, most recently as Dom James' prior, the prospect of guiding a large, dynamic community in an era of dramatic change was not Fr. Flavian's ambition. A vocal advocate of the so-called "hermit movement" within the order, he and Fr. Louis and Father Hilarion Schmock had been the first of the Gethsemani monks to move to the woods. Those who were calling for a revival of the eremitical, or hermit, life argued that it better reflected the "primitive ideal" of monastic life: that is, silence, solitude and seclusion.

Fr. Flavian's election also came at a time when some of his brothers were advocating an alternative to the established system for electing abbots. Rather than election for life, with resignations accepted only when deemed necessary, they proposed the election of abbots for temporary terms: perhaps six years, after which time the community and the abbot would decide whether to continue with the same leadership. Fr. Flavian supported temporary tenures: "I think [as abbot] you know you only have so much to give, and this also allows other people a chance to use their talents." It was with such a reformed system in mind that he made it known he would accept the position if elected.

"I don't know if I could have taken it otherwise. I didn't feel called to be abbot for life," Fr. Flavian recalls today. While he was reluctant to leave the hermitage, he ended up doing so "thinking it would be temporary and I could return to hermit life later. . . . I was paying my dues, doing my service."

Fr. Flavian officially took office at the age of 36, the youngest abbot in Gethsemani's history. He moved out of his hermitage and into the abbot's office in a year that would later be viewed by historians as a turning point in American culture. It was a year branded by televised clashes between police and protesters at the Democratic Convention in Chicago; coast-to-coast campus demonstrations over free speech and civil rights; bloody inner-city riots; and the shocking assassinations of Martin Luther King Jr. and Robert F. Kennedy.

The monastery, despite its strict enclosure, would not be exempt from the disquieting effects of the noise and change outside its walls. News of the anti-war protests of activist nuns and priests, like the Berrigan brothers, filtered into the abbey, where Fr. Louis continued to inspire those outside by writing on issues of peace and race relations from his own perspective.

There is no question there was paradox at work when Gethsemani chose Fr. Flavian, a monk dedicated to the solitary life, to lead the community through such turbulent and precarious times.

FR. FLAVIAN WAS BORN THOMAS BURNS IN JERSEY CITY, New Jersey, on December 23, 1931. His Irish Catholic family put its highest value on marriage and children, and those were his goals growing up. However, he was also greatly influenced in his youth by St. Thérèse of Lisieux and felt a deep attraction to the contemplative life she lived and wrote about so eloquently.

In 1950, not long out of high school, he was living in lower Manhattan, making friends with other young people, most of whom were planning to go to college. His group liked to read the bestsellers at the time, and it so happened that one of the books that came Burns' way that year was Thomas Merton's *The Seven Storey Mountain*. It was Fr. Louis' descriptions of the life at Gethsemani that gave Burns a clue to where he might find the contemplative path that was beckoning him.

His first step was to write a letter to Our Lady of the Valley, a Trappist monastery in nearby Rhode Island.

THE ABBACY OF FATHER FLAVIAN

1968: Father Flavian Burns, a hermit, is elected abbot; Martin Luther King Jr. is assassinated in Memphis; Berrigan brothers and other Catholic priests await arrest after burning hundreds of draft cards; Thomas Merton leaves for extended trip to Asia in October, dies in Bangkok, Thailand, in December.

1969: Man walks on the moon.

1970: Gethsemani takes over a hermit colony in Oxford, North Carolina; National Guardsmen kill four students at Kent State University.

1971: Daniel Ellsberg is indicted for leaking The Pentagon Papers.

1972: Father Flavian announces his desire to resign as abbot.

Top: *Monks getting their hair cut, including Thomas Merton (Father Louis) in center.* Above: *An antiphonary like the ones used by monks in choir before the liturgical changes of the 1960s.*

There he was able to arrange a retreat for the weekend of March 21, the feast of St. Benedict. However, in a portentous turn of events, that monastery was destroyed by fire just before he was to leave for his retreat. Burns' father, who had not been enthusiastic about the direction his oldest son's life was taking, informed him of the monastery's misfortune by holding up a newspaper and pointing to the headline that screamed the bad news. "So," he said solemnly, "do you need a telegram?"

But Burns was not so easily put off. He made new retreat plans – this time at Gethsemani. The fire in Rhode Island was leading him to the place he would call

Above: *A view of the novitiate which now houses the library and archives.* Right: *Booklet commemorating Father Flavian's abbatial blessing.*

ABBATIAL BLESSING

Right Rev. Flavian Burns
Our Lady of Gethsemani Abbey

Feast of Saint Benedict
March 21, 1968

home for over 30 years. (Later, some would also see the incident as a foreshadowing of his 1990 election as abbot at Our Lady of the Holy Cross Abbey in Berryville, Virginia, in the years following his resignation as Gethsemani's abbot. It was, after all, the destruction of Our Lady of the Valley that led to the foundation of St. Joseph Abbey in Spencer, Massachusetts, and ultimately to its daughterhouse at Berryville.)

Burns made his Gethsemani retreat in May around Memorial Day. Though he received no particular encouragement from the monks he encountered in Kentucky, he applied to join the community. He was accepted and entered on January 30, 1951, at the age of 19.

Once inside the cloistered walls, he found a community far different from the one he had read about in Merton's autobiography. He was surprised by the large number of young people, some not as old yet as he. It was a crowded, bustling, active era at Gethsemani, with many young World War II veterans and "Merton converts" infusing the 100-year-old abbey with youthful energy and vitality.

"I expected a few old men walking around with their hoods pulled up. Instead of that, the place was bursting at the seams with youth," Fr. Flavian recalled. "Dom James was abbot just a couple of years then. I think he was the right man for it because first of all he loved youth, and he was willing to accept us into this very staid place and adapt a lot of things gradually for our sake. So it was a lively time. A tough novitiate with 100 novices – but good people, like Chrysogonus Waddell and John Eudes (Bamberger) and James (Conner). Those were some of the people I grew up with. They were all in my novitiate and later in the scholasticate with Father Louis."

Although it was not what he expected, not nearly the version of contemplative life that first had appealed to him through the writings of St. Thérèse, Burns did not look further: "I was convinced I was supposed to be there and so I stayed." During his first few years at Gethsemani, he was "one of the many," according to his own recollection of the period. He studied and was ordained a priest in 1959 at Louisville's Cathedral of the Assumption, after which he "expected to live the quiet life." In his own words, he was "not the most noticeable" young monk in the community.

But that changed in 1960 when Dom James chose him to be among his first monks to study at Gregorian University in Rome. As a result of new rules regarding the education of priests, the Vatican was requiring the abbey to send some of its men for special training in areas such as theology, canon law and Scripture study. "That seemed to change not me, but the way people viewed me," Fr. Flavian said.

He began his European education at the motherhouse in Melleray where he practiced his French. He then moved on to Rome where he studied Canon Law for two years. He returned to Gethsemani with a degree and almost immediately took on new appointments – that of master of scholastics, junior master and, eventually, prior. The busy, people-oriented path Fr. Flavian traveled during the early 1960s was a far cry from the contemplative one which had first attracted him, but it was good preparation for what was to come.

"I ENJOYED BEING ABBOT. GETHSEMANI HAD PLENTY OF people and plenty of talent. As far as I was concerned, the place pretty much ran itself," he would recall 30 years later.

He believed in delegating authority and decided early in his tenure that he would let "the people with talent" run the day-to-day life of the monastery, while he focused on encouraging the spiritual aspects of the life. His emphasis would be on "quieting the place down."

As often was the case in a changing of the guard at Gethsemani, Fr. Flavian was, at least on the surface, a very different personality from that of his predecessor. He was half the age of Dom James, after all. Particularly to the younger monks of Gethsemani, he represented the future. An example of the contrasting styles of the two men is summed up by Brother Paul Quenon, who knew them both:

"When you went to see Dom James, first of all you'd bow, then you'd kneel down by the desk and you'd kiss his ring. And then you would stay kneeling for the whole half hour that you were there. At the end, when you got your blessing, you would kiss his ring and get up and leave.

"But Flavian dropped all of that. You sat down when you talked to Flavian, and you didn't kiss his ring. In fact, Flavian didn't wear a ring. And he didn't wear the pectoral cross, either."

Brother Patrick Hart, who served as his secretary, said Fr. Flavian was the first of Gethsemani's abbots to reject the traditional European title of "Dom" in favor of "Father."

Fr. Flavian was "cooler, more intellectual," according to another observer. His personal preference for contemplative prayer over common chant led him to support the desires of a group of lay brothers who wished to keep saying their "Aves" and "Paters" in private. Following the unification of lay brothers and choir monks, the two groups were expected to pray together in the choir stalls. Fr. Flavian, however, allowed lay brothers to continue their traditional prayers if they wished, a practice that still exists at Gethsemani.

He was an advocate of Vatican II concepts, such as pluralism, and preached in his Chapter talks that the best way for an individual monk to support the community is by following his own unique and personal call from God. It was a message he lived as well as preached.

ONE OF FR. FLAVIAN'S FIRST ACTIONS AS ABBOT WAS to close the gatehouse store, a gift shop that at the time was the point of entry for most visitors. With the support of monks who were assigned to work there, he converted the shop to a reception area so that a newcomer's first impression was not a store stocked with cheese and rosaries for sale. Fr. Flavian also downsized the guesthouse from a full-blown, supervised retreat center, as it had become during Dom James' tenure, to a smaller-scale, quieter place where individuals could come for self-directed retreats.

His goal for the retreat house was simply to "share the quiet of the life" with guests. At the time, the group retreat movement was popular in the Church at large, and so some Catholics in the diocese were disappointed with the change. However, Fr. Flavian believed that there were enough retreat centers run by more active orders to accommodate the groups Gethsemani would no longer serve.

One of his first steps was to give the monks private rooms, rather than the dormitory "cells" that had been a way of life at Gethsemani since its beginning. The only privacy in these small public sleeping places was afforded by a curtain that could be drawn from side to side.

He also expanded the committee structure that Dom James had developed. Under Fr. Flavian, the 125-member community was operating more democratically than ever before. Monks were electing their representatives on the various administrative councils and making their own decisions on pressing issues facing the com-

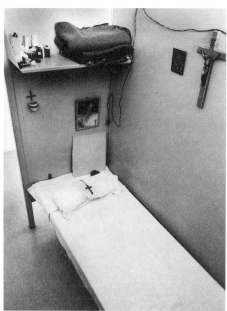

ABOVE: *Under Fr. Flavian, individual cells replaced dormitory cots.*

munity, rather than turning over all responsibility to the abbot. Fr. Flavian did not attend all committee meetings; he believed in delegating authority. However, he did retain veto power over committee decisions.

During this period of great change and experimentation, many lay brothers left Gethsemani. To Fr. Flavian, this was not a crisis peculiar to his abbacy but just one more ebb-and-flow cycle at Gethsemani, a pattern he had observed as a young novice himself and had once dreaded but now saw as an integral part of monastic life.

He liked to tell the story of his own days in the novitiate in the 1950s, when applicants constantly appeared at the gatehouse door. As each new one arrived, he took his place at the end of a row in the choir stalls. When someone left the monastery, the line tightened back up to fill the empty space created by the departure.

Fr. Flavian recalled his uneasiness with that ever-shifting line and the added poignancy it lent to one of the psalms chanted at Compline. It was Psalm 90, whose verses include this prediction: *A thousand will fall at your right and ten thousand will fall at your left, but you it will not touch.* Despite the comfort of those last few words, the psalm raised a lingering fear in the young novice's mind that he might "fall" along with the others. "You had this anxiety all through the novitiate that you wouldn't make it," he said. And many of his era did not. "But that's been the history of Gethsemani," he said. "People came and went."

Some monks viewed the glut of departures during Fr. Flavian's tenure in another light. As they saw it, Dom James had not been an easy man to approach with doubts about one's vocation. When he resigned and became a hermit, some who had been discouraged from

179

leaving by Dom James now turned to his successor, who believed this decision like most others was their responsibility, not his, to make.

IN JULY 1972, FOUR AND A HALF YEARS INTO HIS "temporary" abbacy, Fr. Flavian made it known he wanted to return to his hermitage in the woods. He suggested a series of community meetings on the topic of his resignation. If a majority believed his departure would damage Gethsemani, he would delay it.

According to minutes of those meetings, Fr. Flavian was praised for his efforts to quiet down the monastery and re-emphasize the Cistercian ideal of simplicity. His detached style of leadership was, in the eyes of many, balanced by his willingness to be available for counsel with any monk at any time.

But he persisted in his efforts to return to the woods: "There were plenty of people who could be abbot, but not too many wanted to be a hermit. I felt being a hermit might be my more important contribution to Gethsemani and to the world."

In October, during Gethsemani's annual visitation, Dom Columban of Melleray personally posed the question of Fr. Flavian's resignation to every monk he interviewed. Two-thirds did not believe it would damage the community. Fr. Flavian's request was then approved by the Abbot General with input from the abbots of all Gethsemani's daughterhouses.

His resignation was made official on January 31, 1973. Six weeks later, the community elected Father Timothy Kelly to succeed him, and it was back to the hermitage for Fr. Flavian.

"Timothy let me live pretty much the way I wanted to. I had contact with the community. I had people coming out regularly. It was a nice set-up. I went in for professions, ordinations, Christmas, Easter. . . . I had time to live what I considered the contemplative life. I was very happy and ready to spend the rest of my life there," Fr. Flavian recalled.

But that's not how it turned out. In 1980 Fr. Flavian's good friend, Dom Edward McCorkell of Berryville, was considering retirement. He, too, felt a call to the hermit life. He turned to Fr. Flavian for counsel. "I encouraged him," Fr. Flavian recalled. "I said, 'You did your part. You want to be a hermit and lead the quiet life now. I think you should feel free to do that.' Little did I realize he had it in mind for me to be his successor."

So, once again, Fr. Flavian was running a monastery, this time at Berryville, where he served as temporary superior nearly five years.

In 1984, he returned to his Gethsemani hermitage. A year and a half later, he was called to be temporary superior at the Trappist monastery in Ava, Missouri. Two years after that, he was back to his Gethsemani hermitage. After a year and a half, the monks of Berryville elected him their abbot. He served six years, then resigned in 1996 to become chaplain of a Trappistine convent in Crozet, Virginia. He now lives a quiet life in a small two-story house on the convent grounds. In recent years, he transferred his vow of stability from Gethsemani to Berryville, where he said "they need me more." In the fall of 1997, he explained his life at Crozet this way:

"Berryville has the obligation to supply chaplains to this convent. All I have to do is say Mass for the nuns and occasionally help them out making their cheese. They know I'm trying to live the hermit life." He does not know how long he will stay there: "I've stopped planning my future."

Although the concept of temporary abbots did not become the rule among Trappists, there is now a vote before each election to determine whether the abbot will serve a six-year term or an "indefinite" one. Fr. Timothy, for instance, is now serving an "indefinite" term. Fr. Flavian, on the other hand, still advocates shorter tenures: "I think everywhere I've been abbot, I won't say I've been successful, but I've been well-received and liked. The only thing they don't like about me is I don't stay. Because I don't believe in it."

Today, Fr. Flavian is at peace with the back-and-forth path his monastic vocation has followed: "I hope the Lord is as happy with my life as I have been." When he looks back to his first monastery, the Abbey of Gethsemani, it is always with "great affection."

"It's a very accepting community. I think it can be because it's large. People come there from different countries, different places. . . . But it also has continuity. When you live at a place like Gethsemani, you are conscious, even in the woods, of the monks who have lived there. We stripped the place during my lifetime and saw the bricks they made, how they built the place eight bricks thick.

"I think it's a place in America where people could go on pilgrimage, so to speak. It's a holy place. That's the way I felt when I went there, and that's the way I still feel about it. "

HERMIT LIFE at GETHSEMANI

IT WAS A SIGN OF THE TIMES, A HINT OF WHAT WAS IN the air, a clue to the coming decade.

In January 1968, the monks of Gethsemani experienced a changing of the guard. Dom James Fox was moving out of the abbot's office that he had occupied for 20 years, into a hermitage perched on a remote hillside miles out from the abbey. Fr. Flavian Burns was moving into the abbot's office, leaving behind the solitary life he had been living in a cottage in the woods for the previous year and a half.

An abbot turned hermit, and a hermit turned abbot. It was a situation unheard of in Gethsemani's history. In the context of the day, however, it was fitting and hardly a surprise.

Faced with electing a successor to the abbot who had led Gethsemani through its most active and change-filled era to date, the community chose a monk who had made it clear that he felt called to live alone, in simplicity, without the support of traditional Cistercian life.

What did this change of course portend? The answer to that question is a story of experimentation and lessons learned, of distant huts on foreign soil and "hippie communes" as neighbors, of a yearning for balance, of a return to primitive ideals, of the ebb and flow of monastic culture and the inevitable, unwavering swing of the pendulum.

LET US SKIP FORWARD A FEW YEARS.

It is December 1976, eight years after the sudden death of Thomas Merton and more than a decade after his long-delayed and much-documented move to a hermitage. On Christmas Day that year, seven of Merton's Gethsemani brothers were living some form of the hermit life he had pioneered.

Four monks occupied hermitages on monastery property: two former abbots, Dom James and Fr. Flavian, and Fr. Hilarion and Brother Lavrans Nielsen. Two other monks, both priests, had moved abroad: Fr. Matthew Kelty to a hut in New Guinea where he stayed 10 years, and Father Roman Ginn to a poor area of Mexico for 19 years. One older monk, Father Alfons Berg, lived as a hermit within his own monastery cell.

What was happening at Gethsemani was part of an international renewal of interest. Its leaders were fervent, but few in number. In 1967, throughout the Order, there were only seven monks worldwide living as hermits on Trappist property. Another nine lived elsewhere, often in remote locations far from their communities. It was reported in the minutes of the General Chapter that year that "very few superiors seem opposed in principle to this little eremitical movement within the Order."

Yet, by the mid-1970s, the movement had gained

cated the hermit life as a special vocation of his generation of Trappists, objected to regulating it with laws.

In some ways, 1976 was the peak of the hermit movement at Gethsemani, the beginning of a slow but steady decline in interest and support. Today there are only three hermit monks, all living on monastery property.

Fr. Roman, who returned from Mexico in 1990, now lives in a small cottage. Fr. Chrysogonus Waddell lives in the hermitage originally built for Fr. Flavian. Fr. Hilarion lives in a large trailer in a wooded area not far from Fr. Flavian's hermitage.

Others, searching for greater solitude but not wishing to live alone, improvise within the confines of community life. For 30 years, Father Alan Gilmore has maintained within the enclosure a daytime hermitage

ABOVE: *Father Matthew's hermitage.* RIGHT: *St. Anne's, an abandoned toolshed used as a daytime hermitage by Merton before he received permission to live full time as a hermit.*

enough momentum to prompt the Cistercian Order to consider a statute that would legislate exactly who could be a Trappist hermit and how they could go about being one. The proposal had little support at Gethsemani, however. The new abbot, Fr. Timothy, had taken a clear stand on the subject: he believed hermits were detrimental to the Cistercian vocation and its fundamental focus on community. "By nature or by grace, I am somewhat anti-hermit," he wrote. Even Fr. Flavian, who advo-

that he named St. Aidan's Anchorage. The small frame shelter that once functioned as a pig sty on land where sows birthed their young today serves as a quiet place for prayer and reflection. More recently, Br. Paul Quenon has taken to spending his nights sleeping in the corner of an open woodshed. And Merton's first hermitage, a shed he called St. Anne's, has been restored by a monk who now uses it as a retreat by day.

What is it that leads a monk to a path detached from

Father Roman Ginn grew up in Denver, Colorado, and spent World War II playing trumpet in a band with some of the rising stars of the swing era. He was stationed in Rio de Janeiro when the U.S. dropped the atom bomb. After a year on

his own playing in Brazil, he decided that, for him, "the musician's life is no life." So he sold his trumpet to "the best player in Rio," and headed home.

In 1946, he entered Gethsemani and studied for a time in Rome. But he felt called to a path of greater solitude than the community life could offer. In 1966, he spent six years at Gethsemani's daughterhouse in Chile. For three of those years, he lived as a hermit in the foothills of the Andes. His only companion was a 20-year old mule.

Soon after his return to Gethsemani in 1972, he left again to live as a hermit in Mexico, in a hermitage perched so high in the mountains he could spot rain 30 miles away.

In 1990, he returned to Gethsemani and took up residence in a remote setting several miles out from the monastery. He lives there now in a primitive one-room cabin on a patch of land he shares with two donkeys, Hosanna and Hallelujah. He cooks outdoors and keeps his perishables safe in a root cellar outside his door. He plants and harvests his own garden, which typically includes crops of kale, turnips, beans and squash. He supplements these vegetables with staples such as coffee, rice, Crystal Light and peanut butter that he picks up at the monastery on his Sunday visits. He makes his weekly trips on foot, pulling the supplies in his Radio Flyer.

"I'm not here to produce," he says of the solitary life he has led for three decades, "I'm here to be."

his brothers, disconnected from the conventional routines of Trappist life? Merton wrote plenty on the subject, but perhaps no words of his better describe the appeal of a hermitage than this journal passage dated February 25, 1965:

I can imagine no other joy on earth than to have such a place to be at peace in, to live in silence, to think and write, to listen to the wind and all the voices of the wood, to live in the shadow of the big cedar cross, to prepare for my death and my exodus to the heavenly country, to love my brothers and all people, and to pray for the whole world and for peace and good sense among men.

THE MODERN HERMIT MOVEMENT, WHICH HAD ITS beginnings in the Order during the 1950s, picked up steam in the 1960s as post-Vatican II reforms opened the doors to experimentation within the Church. There was lively debate about the role of hermits in modern monastic life, and support for its revival came from important quarters. The concept of monks living away from their monasteries in solitude, or living as hermits in close physical proximity (what is variously called a *laura,* a *skete* or a grange) took on a life of its own. Experimental monasteries were proposed and founded by various orders. By 1964, Dom Jacques Winandy, a Benedictine monk, had published a *Manual for Hermits,* which roughly outlined the way he and his Hermits of St. John the Baptist lived together in a Canadian community.

Later in the decade, the push for "hermit colonies" gained support from writers such as Father Peter Minard and Dom Jean Leclercq, both Benedictines, and Dom Andre Louf, a Cistercian. Like Merton, these men were writing articles, corresponding with one another and attending conferences, advocating their position.

Years before his move to the woods and subsequent election as abbot, Fr. Flavian had approached Dom James, asking to join a small group of monks from various countries who were hoping to live as hermits under the guidance of a retired abbot. When that was turned down, he and some of his Gethsemani brothers, including Fr. Louis, developed plans for a group of hermits to live separately but nearby one another on an unused tract of monastery property. Everett Edelin, a neighbor and friend of the abbey, had donated the land, which led to its nickname, "The Garden of Edelin." The land went by many other names as well, including Edelin's Hollow and Keith Hollow, local names for the site. In a letter to Dom James, in March 1966, Fr. Flavian had suggested that the Edelin project begin that spring or summer.

That request was denied in 1966, but not all was lost in the venture. Fr. Flavian was given a private hermitage instead – to his surprise: "Dom James was shrewd. I didn't know at the time that he had it in his own mind to go to a hermitage." But the signs had long been there. Once skeptical of its relevance to the Trappist way, Dom James eventually spoke of the hermit vocation as a "fruit of community life" and an organic element of Cistercian tradition. For support, he referred to a 12th-century monk named Roger, who was allowed by his abbot to live alone 13 miles out from the Abbey of St. Alban.

The possibility of a hermit colony arose again at Gethsemani in 1970, when Fr. Flavian presented his council with a proposal to take over an experimental monastery founded by Father Meinrad on 30 acres of woodland near Oxford, North Carolina. The monastery, according to minutes of the council meeting, consisted of several small buildings, a mobile home unit, a 1968 Chevy, a kitty of about $14,000 and (most important to the monks who supported taking it over) the answer to a vocational prayer.

In 1970, with community approval, three monks of Gethsemani left for Oxford on the Feast of St. John the Baptist. Life there was simple and austere. The hermit monks wore no habits, allowed no music and supported themselves by weaving. Fr. Matthew Kelty was there the longest, staying until November 1973, when he set out for New Guinea and an even more primitive life.

Throughout the 1970s, proposals for hermit colonies cropped up in the community. About the time Gethsemani took over Oxford, Br. Frederic Collins resurrected the idea of a grange at Keith Hollow, and it was debated by Fr. Flavian's council well into 1972.

That same year, a professor from nearby Berea College asked the abbey to allow a community of spiritually oriented individuals – some married, some single, some with children – to live together on a 20-acre plot of unused monastery land. The group proposed to live as much as possible by the Rule of St. Benedict and to cultivate close ties to the abbey. The Gethsemani community, as a whole, didn't support the idea, however. Perhaps put off by fears of a "hippie commune" on their land, the monks turned down the request.

The Families of St. Benedict, as they called themselves, moved instead to a 105-acre farm a few miles from the monastery. Though unconnected to the abbey in any official way, the group lived a life modeled on Cistercian principles, involving communal prayer, voluntary poverty and contemplation. They stayed on the land for about 12 years and maintained their ties to Gethsemani through Brother Frederic, who met with them regularly as a kind of monastery liaison.

"I went out there once a week to their meetings and to pass on to them something about monasticism," he said. "They were very idealistic – into poverty and simplicity. Over the years there were 30 people who came and went through that community. We became very good friends."

In 1973, at the time of Fr. Timothy's election, the proposal for a grange at Gethsemani was still being discussed. Council meeting minutes show that 10 monks were interested in reviving the project on the Edelin property, not far from Dom James' hermitage. Fr. Flavian had parked a trailer on the land while he was still abbot, with the idea that, should the plan be approved, he would preside over the other hermit monks. This plan was based on a proposal Fr. Louis had written for Dom James years earlier, with the same piece of property in mind.

Ultimately, however, the plan failed to gain enough support from the new abbot or the community. So instead of presiding over a *skete,* Fr. Flavian returned to his private hermitage. Eventually the community decided to pull out of the Oxford experiment as well, allowing another monastery to take it over. The push for alternative small communities faded at Gethsemani and eventually throughout the Order.

THE URGE TO ESTABLISH HERMIT COLONIES IS CYCLICAL, Fr. Flavian believes: "In my time we were going back to the sources. We realized the first Cistercians left the established monasteries and lived in primitive situations. . . . If you read the history, there's always this desire to return to the primitive ideal. But it's not very realistic, so it doesn't last. You have to have almost a saint in charge in order to do it. But when that saint dies, there's no one left to carry it on."

Even the "solitary hermit" movement faded out after a while. Today the Gethsemani landscape is littered with abandoned hermitages, grown over with brush and in severe disrepair, including Dom James' cottage on the hill and Br. Lavrans' brown brick studio.

Perhaps it was the intense activity of the 1950s at Gethsemani, with its numerous noisy construction projects and its burgeoning mail-order business, that prompted some monks to seek balance in seclusion. With the "quieting down" of Fr. Flavian's abbacy, and the settling in of post-Vatican II reforms, the yearning for physical separation and undiluted solitude may have subsided. At least for a while.

In a 1965 letter to Dom Basiolio Penido of Brazil, Merton struck a prophetic note about this unorthodox way of life he advocated so passionately:

The hermit experiment is being looked at with a certain favor now in some monasteries, but I think there will inevitably be disappointments if too much is expected.

"INTO the REALM of LIGHT"

ABOVE: *Woodcut of Jesus with the woman at the well.* RIGHT: *Brother Lavrans Nielsen and his work.*

THE ART OF BR. LAVRANS NIELSEN IS TODAY AS MUCH A part of the landscape of Gethsemani as are its wooded knobs and gently rolling fields.

Br. Lavrans' haunting icons, executed in the Greek and Russian styles, set the stage for quiet reflection in the retreat house, where guest room walls bear their reproductions. His grand liturgical banners, towering over the abbey altar on feast days, lend an awesome grace to that deep, distant space. His linoleum block prints animate Christmas greetings and holy cards. His woodcuts, engravings and calligraphy illuminate texts. His abstract oil paintings, distinguished by their layers of three-dimensional light, speak with wisdom and uncommon wit.

Br. Lavrans (born Donald Anthony Nielsen in Brooklyn, New York) entered Gethsemani in 1957, at the age of 20. During Fr. Flavian's tenure as abbot, Br. Lavrans moved into a brick hermitage built just outside the cloister, close enough for visitors to view his work. Alone in the large studio space designed specifically to accommodate his massive canvases and banners, Br. Lavrans – an entirely self-educated artist – created an amazingly diverse body of work.

By 1970, he had exhibited at the J.B. Speed Museum in Louisville and later had shows throughout the region. In 1975, responding to work on display at the Swearingen-Byck Gallery in Louisville, *Courier-Journal* art critic Sarah Lansdell remarked: "Brother Lavrans is launching farther and deeper into a realm of light and texture. His paintings are surely extraordinary experiences *in the painting;* they are certainly remarkable experiences in the seeing."

The following year, Br. Lavrans left the Trappists. At the age of 40, he moved to

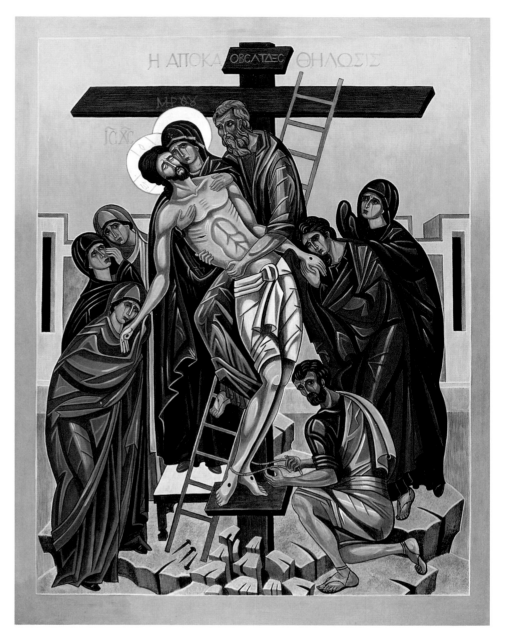

Atlanta, where he continued to paint in the style of abstract expressionism. In 1991, he died. Much of his work remains at the abbey, as does the memory of his gracious spirit.

The following is an excerpt from a homily written by Fr. Matthew Kelty, entitled *Remembering Lavrans,* delivered on August 30, 1991, at Gethsemani:

It is rather interesting to note the rather droll way in which Lavrans' monastic career in art actually began. His assignment one season was to operate the vacuum machine that drew the air from plastic sacks of quartered cheese rounds and then sealed them. It was, of course, a monotonous routine that would drive a man like Lavrans into a state of high exasperation. This went on for some time, until he began to break out in large, ugly boils. A halt was called and the brother in charge made a bold move, offering to Lavrans the following deal. If Lavrans would milk the cows each morning – no favorite among mostly city monks – and do the related chores, he could have the afternoon for his art. Lavrans seized the opportunity. This marked the first time any monk had been given official work time for something like art.

TOP LEFT: *Woodcut of Jesus in the Garden of Gethsemani.*
ABOVE: *Icon of Jesus being taken down from the cross.*
RIGHT: *Woodcut of Eve picking the apple.*

A MONK'S LEGACY: THE LIFE and DEATH of FATHER LOUIS

DURING THE FIRST YEAR OF FR. FLAVIAN'S TENURE AS abbot, an event occurred that profoundly changed Gethsemani. It was as dramatic an occurrence as any in the monastery's history. It stands today as the event most often linked to his time in office.

The event was, of course, the death of Thomas Merton, the monastery's best-known monk and Fr. Flavian's close friend and fellow hermit. They had worked side by side after Fr. Flavian's return from Rome, when they both were assigned to the novices.

"We were collaborators," said Fr. Flavian. "I was certainly his choice to be abbot. To some extent, it was . . . like himself getting elected, like him getting the job. Part of the reason I was able to accept it was that I thought I would have him to rely on."

Michael Mott, author of *The Seven Mountains of Thomas Merton,* describes in that biography a meeting held at Fr. Louis' hermitage on Christmas Day 1967. Jokingly referred to as a "General Chapter of Hermits," it included Fr. Flavian, Fr. Hilarion and Merton. Mott writes: "When Father Louis poured out the wine, he managed a trickle in Father Hilarion's glass, a trickle in his own, then almost spilled the wine, overfilling Father Flavian's glass. This, he claimed, was a clear sign Father Flavian would be chosen."

Portrait of Father Louis (Thomas Merton) by John Howard Griffin.

In the end, Fr. Flavian assured Merton he would accept the abbot's job if elected. A few weeks later, on January 13, 1968, the community voted him in as abbot.

It was later that year, in October, that Merton left the monastery on the trip that would ultimately take him to Bangkok, Thailand, and his death. The two did not have much contact during Merton's travels through Asia, according to Fr. Flavian: "I was busy while he was away. In one of his letters to Br. Patrick, he teases: 'I wrote to Flavian and he hasn't answered me yet.'"

When news of Merton's death reached the monastery, Fr. Flavian and Br. Patrick Hart immediately set to work, trying to locate those who would be invited to the funeral. (Coincidentally the news arrived on December 10, the anniversary of Merton's arrival at Gethsemani in 1941 and also Dom James' birthday.) Fr. Flavian struggled with logistical problems posed by a death so far from home. He wanted an autopsy performed but was warned that such a procedure, under prevailing Thai regulations, would require Merton to be buried in Thailand. His body was instead retrieved from local authorities who agreed to hand it over only after they were told it was needed for a religious ceremony.

Once the body was in the hands of Catholic authorities at the conference, the U.S. Embassy placed the body in the bay of an SAC bomber and sent it home. In California, it was transferred to a commercial airliner. All along the way, there were delays. The burial and funeral took place Tuesday, December 17, a full week after Fr. Louis was electrocuted by a fan in his Bangkok room.

"Merton was late for his own funeral," Fr. Flavian said. "We didn't get the body until after the funeral was to start. We had all these people on our hands. We just had to wait." Once in Kentucky, Merton's body was taken to New Haven, Kentucky, where Fr. Flavian was called to identify his dear friend.

While the outside world reacted with grief and shock, Fr. Flavian wrote a homily he preached to his community the day after Merton's death. "I think I spoke for the whole community when I gave that homily. Fortunately I had good inspiration for it."

There was never any doubt in Fr. Flavian's mind that Fr. Louis, long after death, would continue to influence his monastery, his order and his church. "Father Louis made Gethsemani what it is," he said. "But all monasteries, not just Gethsemani, flourished because of Merton. His death, by happy divine providence, hasn't lessened his effect."

He has left his mark deep in this community, and it will be with us for years to come, for he has planted it in the hearts of a generation, and God willing, it will be planted again for generations to come. Each of you, I am sure, would read his message somewhat differently and this, of course, is the way he would have it. But the message is basically the same for all. We are men of God only insofar as we are seeking God and only insofar as we find Him in the truth about ourselves. Silence, solitude, and seclusion are

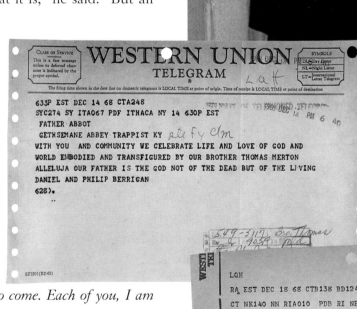

Photograph of Father Louis (Thomas Merton) in priest garb, taken by Jay Laughlin, his friend and publisher.

means to this and nothing more. The end of all is purity of faith and love, and the thing that keeps us going is our hope.

 –Fr. Flavian Burns in a homily the day after
  Fr. Louis' death

You could tell Father Louis by his walk. He had a rather rapid walk, but not altogether measured and orderly. For one thing, his feet were spread out fan-fashion, and there was something sad in his gait. But it was a vigorous walk, except when he was reading, as he often was. He had small hands and feet (he was very hard on shoes!) and a fine torso with strong shoulders and back. His legs seemed a bit short and this made him look smaller than he really was. Clothes did not suit him well: I mean he never looked neat and spruce, though in his monk's habit he was presentable enough. Things rather hung on him and some-how looked baggy and shapeless. Even when dressed in civilian clothes, he did not look sharp, but a trifle disordered and disorganized. He did not care much about clothes, that was obvious.

 –Fr. Matthew Kelty in *Thomas Merton Monk*

He was anything but a "team man" and submission to a superior was considerably less connatural to him than, say, flying, planeless, in the air. There always remained a certain ill-defined, latent air of daring about him that conveyed the distinct impression of unpredictability. A quality that led one to feel, "What might he do next?" His temperament, at once energetic and gregarious, and his broad and varied culture made the most diverse kind of international society congenial to him. It turned out that, even though Bardstown is some-what removed from the American mainline for foreign visitors, there was a steady stream of persons of multifarious interests coming to speak with him from all over the world. He counted among his friends Vietnamese Buddhists, Hindu monks, Japanese Zen masters, Sufi mystics, professors of reli-

gion and mysticism from Jerusalem's University, French philosophers, artists and poets from Europe, South America, and the States, Arabic scholars, Mexican sociologists and many others.

 –Fr. John Eudes Bamberger, Abbot of Genesee, in
  Thomas Merton Monk

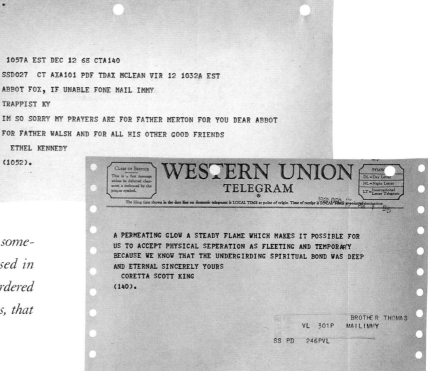

Being a brother of Fr. Louis, Thomas Merton, I think I have some sense of what he hoped for from the Merton collection. One thing he did not want was a monument. He might just be a little embarrassed with what we are doing today. What he did want, and what hopefully is being provided by this ample and well appointed facility, is that others would have access to his work – primarily as an encouragement to enter their personal journey, seeking the truth, seeking God. He wanted known the many revelations of the circuitous route that he took, so that none of us would be discouraged by all that overwhelms us. He wanted us to know and find hope in that.

 –Remarks made by Abbot Timothy Kelly at the
  dedication of the Merton Center in October 1997

FATHER TIMOTHY KELLY:
OUT of the FRONT OFFICE,
INTO the STREET
1973-

OPPOSITE: *An aerial view of Gethsemani, looking east.* ABOVE: *A madonna and child, sculpted by Peter Watts, now located in the abbey cloister.*

W HEN DOM JAMES FOX AIR-CONDITIONED THE abbey church during the renovations of the mid-1960s, not all of his monks approved. One of those who objected was Father Timothy Kelly, a young Canadian choir monk who was studying in Rome at the time. Though neither man could have known it then, their disagreement over the air conditioner was much more than a clash of opinions over the appropriate room temperature for a Trappist church.

Within a decade, Fr. Timothy himself would be presiding over the community as its eighth abbot. If nothing else, the story of the disputed air conditioner foreshadows the contrast in style and philosophy of Gethsemani's two most influential modern-day abbots.

A New Englander who never adjusted to Kentucky's sweltering summers, and an unabashed fan of American technology, Dom James viewed the air-conditioning of the abbey church as a practical necessity, not a spiritual matter. He was so sure of the rightness of his decision that he had the equipment installed without consulting his community. He quickly learned, however, that to some of his men, air conditioning was a convenience totally unbefitting Trappist life. Fr. Matthew Kelty well remembers the barrage of complaints and the abbot's response to them.

"They said, 'The Garden of Gethsemani – air-conditioned? Oh, come and pray with Jesus in comfort!' But Dom James said, 'They'll all pray more if the place is air-conditioned.' And they said, 'What kind of prayer is that, if you sit in the church because it's cool?' Oh, it was very nasty."

From Rome, Fr. Timothy wrote letters objecting to the air conditioner. Looking back, he remembers being concerned about certain attitudes that had crept into the Church in the wake of Vatican II. There was, as he saw it, a growing "uncritical acceptance" of elements of contemporary culture, particularly its material conve-

niences. In his opinion, too many Catholic leaders – including monastic ones – were condemning "everything old as wrong" and welcoming "anything new in the culture as helpful." While he supported Council reforms that encouraged the Church to embrace the world, he feared that some went overboard. The air-conditioning of a Cistercian church seemed to him a perfect example of the latter.

By the time the matter came to light, however, there was little anyone could do about it, least of all Fr. Timothy who was thousands of miles away in another country. As Fr. Matthew recalls, the air conditioner caught the community off-guard. He remembers the day (and the way) he and his brothers found out about it:

"Halfway through the renovation, this enormous big engine arrived – a vat packed in a wooden case –

and the monks were all wondering, in sign language, *What's this machine? An ice machine? For the church! For the house of God!* Oh, my, they were indignant. They didn't want it."

Fr. Matthew was on the abbot's council at the time. He says the group decided not to fight the air conditioner. They felt it didn't make that much difference. So, summer after summer, for the rest of Dom James' time in office and throughout Fr. Flavian's as well, the air conditioner cooled the church.

"It was awful," recalls Br. Paul Quenon. "The place was too cold. It was like walking into an ice box and walking out of it again. I didn't like it." But it was not the temperature that bothered him most. It was what air conditioning represented: "Materially, Dom James was in favor of the American way of life, while a lot of the rest of us were reacting against it."

For the most part, however, the controversy faded.

Then, in 1973, after his election as abbot, Fr. Timothy did what he had been wanting to do for years. He turned off the air conditioner. "I did it right away," he recalls today, laughing at the memory. "It made me real popular."

Oddly enough, in the long run, it *was* a popular decision. The community decided to send the money it saved by turning off the equipment to Mother Teresa of Calcutta to support her charitable work in India. Today, 25 years and many a sweltering August later, the air conditioner is still turned off.

Occasionally one of his monks will bring up the issue, usually in a teasing way, according to Fr. Timothy. "One of the brothers will say to me, 'What are you going to do when your successor turns it back on?' 'Enjoy it,' I

say, 'just like the rest of you.' "

But the abbot stands by his decision and the monastic philosophy it reflects. "Any serious spiritual life needs a certain discipline and a sort of penance, just the ordinary kind that comes from living every day," Fr. Timothy says.

Then, laughing, he reveals a glimpse of his practical side and a hint of his wry sense of humor: "I often say to them now, 'You'd be working 40 hours a week to pay the electricity if you were air-conditioning that thing.' "

But also woven into the fabric of this story are strands of Fr. Timothy's developing philosophy of leadership. Personal responsibility and community consultation – cornerstones of his abbacy – were clearly already at work in the young monk who did not hesitate to lodge a protest, even from afar, when his abbot acted without first conferring with his brothers.

THERE ARE MANY WORDS THAT APTLY DESCRIBE THE eighth abbot of Gethsemani. Energetic. Trusting. Modest. Democratic. Accessible. Sympathetic. A good listener. An instinctual leader.

But the word that best describes him during his early years at Gethsemani is that of "dissenter." The story of the abbey air conditioner is but one example. Long before that conflict arose, well before he left for Europe to study canon law, Fr. Timothy had voiced general concerns about Dom James' renovation project as a whole.

"I would have been more for a restoration than a renovation. I just had a lot different perception of what it should be," he recalls. "Others agreed, but Dom James didn't allow us to speak up much, and he was a good salesman." Consequently, the abbot's plans went through without a hitch.

Fr. Timothy and other critics of the renovation questioned the expenditure of so much money, time and energy on a major overhaul of the monastery when they felt something less radical might have been sufficient. They were also concerned about the noise and commotion it would create. That was a valid concern, as it turned out. As Father Alan Gilmore recalls, life at Gethsemani during the renovation was "like living in a beaten drum."

Fr. Timothy was not shy about expressing his reservations, nor was his abbot timid in his response to them. "I had a number of observations to make," Fr. Timothy remembers, "and so it was thought that perhaps I had too much to say."

LEFT: *Documents from the mid-1960s, when Fr. Timothy studied in Rome at Gregorian University.* ABOVE: *A view of the renovation work at the monastery during the same period.*

And so it was, in the fall of 1965 Fr. Timothy was sent to Rome. He earned his degree there in 1967 and fully expected at that time to return to Kentucky. But Dom James told him to stay in Rome a little longer. Fr. Timothy obeyed his abbot and signed up for further study in moral theology. He was still in Europe when, later that year, Dom James announced his intentions to resign and become a hermit.

Despite his youth, Fr. Timothy was one of those whose names were mentioned as possible successor to Dom James. At 32, he had already emerged as a leader in the community. In fact, one reason he was sent to Rome to study, he later learned from Dom James, was for preparation to head up future foundations.

In keeping with Gethsemani's make-do frontier tradition, however, Fr. Timothy's training as a leader had been informal, almost casual. When asked today about his grooming for the ultimate monastery job, he affirms that "it was all by the seat of my pants." Yet the effect of certain early influences was surely profound. As undermaster to Merton's master of novices, for example, Fr. Timothy witnessed first hand the power of the artful voice of dissent and the crucial change it provokes in a place and its people over time.

"When I heard Dom James was resigning, I wrote him a letter," Fr. Timothy recalls. By now, his visa had expired and in order to come home, he needed Dom James to send certain personal documents required for renewal. But months went by without an answer to his letter. A week before the election, Dom James finally responded. He apologized for the delay, saying he had just found Fr. Timothy's request on his desk.

"Well, I couldn't do anything then," Fr. Timothy recalls with a smile. "So I wrote on a piece of paper, 'YOU WIN.'"

He finally made it home in mid-1968, after Fr. Flavian supplied the necessary documents. Looking back, Fr. Timothy believes his time in Rome benefited him – and his brothers at Gethsemani – in two ways. First, he was able to personally experience the Second Vatican Council, meeting some of the key players of that dynamic period and hearing for himself some of the critical discussions. "I was basically a conservative person," he recalls. "To see the Church in that context opened my eyes. It was a blessing in disguise."

The second reason Fr. Timothy believes it was good for him to go to Rome speaks directly to the old Cistercian wisdom about the right abbot coming along at the right time.

"Some people were pushing that I become abbot after Dom James. I think that would have been a horrendous mistake because, at that time, I would have tried to still be a lot like him in some ways. Fr. Flavian [was better suited] to make a corrective to what had gone before. He was the ideal person to make that transition."

But Fr. Flavian would lead the community for only five years. By the time of his resignation, Fr. Timothy was clearly ready for the challenges of the post-Vatican II era.

THE YEAR THAT GETHSEMANI ELECTED DOM FREDERIC Dunne as its first American abbot – 1935 – was also the year that its first Canadian abbot was born. Patrick Joseph Kelly entered this world on May 26, 1935, in a little town called Amherstburg on the Detroit River in Ontario, Canada. He was the youngest of five children born to Thomas Irving Kelly and his wife, Monica – or Mona, as she was known to family and friends.

Although Fr. Timothy's grandfather was an Irish immigrant, the family did not retain much of an attachment to Ireland or its customs. And while he spontaneously describes his family as "religious," he qualifies it by adding, "but not really pious." All three Kelly sons entered the priesthood, while both daughters married and raised families.

Mr. Kelly was a lighthouse keeper on the Detroit River. Fr. Timothy is quick to point out, however, that "it wasn't a romantic lighthouse, it was the opposite — more of a traffic light for lake freighters." His father also was involved with a company that supplied ships with linens and food. Fr. Timothy remembers the lighthouse fondly as a "quiet place . . . in the middle of the river" where he and his siblings liked to swim and play on summer days.

Mona Kelly was a home-maker until her husband's death in 1965, when she took a job as housemother for a student dormitory on the University of Windsor campus. Both parents strongly opposed their youngest son's early attraction to the contemplative life, but it was Mona Kelly who would put up the biggest fight to keep him in Canada, where she was convinced he belonged.

But that's getting ahead of the story.

Sometime before his high school graduation in 1953, young Pat Kelly told both his parents that he felt called to the life at Gethsemani. They were not entirely surprised by this announcement. As a teenager, he had made a high-school retreat at Gethsemani, and his curiosity about monasticism had only grown stronger in the interim.

Nevertheless, his parents urged him to try something else — anything else — and so upon his graduation he entered the novitiate run by the Congregation of Priests of St. Basil at Richmond Hill near Toronto. This was the order his brother belonged to, as well as the one that had operated the schools and parishes he attended

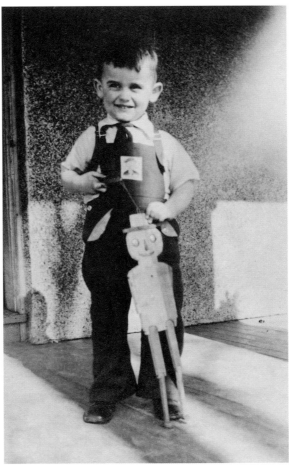

Fr. Timothy as a child in his hometown of Amherstburg, Ontario.

as a boy. It was familiar territory, but not where he heard God's call. He stayed long enough to earn a bachelor of arts degree in philosophy and history and begin studies for the priesthood.

Then, on June 9, 1958, with the approval of his spiritual director at the seminary, he wrote a formal letter of application to Gethsemani. He was 23 years old at the time, "a sensible, steady, conscientious and industrious young man with better than average ability," according to the letter of recommendation sent to Gethsemani's abbot by one of Fr. Timothy's seminary teachers.

Mona Kelly took a different tack in the letter she wrote to Dom James on June 16, 1958, one week after her son's application to Gethsemani. In her handwritten, strongly worded appeal, Mrs. Kelly begged the abbot to "please refuse" her son.

"Yesterday Patrick J. Kelly C.S.B. came down and told his Dad his plans," she wrote. "Well, he never approved of contemplative communities and nearly died when Pat went to Kentucky for a retreat five years ago. Do not tell Pat I have written but please send him back. I am positive if he goes for good in September, it will kill his Dad."

In the bottom corner of her letter, she scribbled: "Please no answer. Act — that is all."

As requested, the abbot did not answer her letter — but neither did he act. Meanwhile, on August 28, Fr. Timothy left Canada for good to become a Trappist of

Gethsemani. One month later, to the day, Mrs. Kelly wrote a second letter to Dom James.

"Without a doubt, it has been the longest month we ever spent. Mr. Kelly is really heartbroken and will never be reconciled to contemplative life," she wrote this time. "Please watch this boy (he is or *was* in perfect health) for any sign of physical illness or mental break down. We are nearly crazy with worry."

Dom James, who had been traveling in Europe that summer and early fall, finally responded to Mrs. Kelly with a letter dated November 6. His tone is cordial but firm. One can only guess how she felt about it. Their dialogue ends with his letter, as far as the abbey archives are concerned. There is no evidence of further correspondence between the two.

"It was a wonderful privilege to receive another charming letter from you signed, 'Pat's Mother,' " Dom James begins his letter to Mrs. Kelly. After explaining his delay, he moves on to tell her how lucky she is to have a son in a Trappist monastery and how smooth the adjustment has been for him: "How many mothers would give all they have just to have a son at Gethsemani. He is so strong looking and sturdy, and he always has a smile."

Apparently hoping to establish rapport with Mrs. Kelly, Dom James shares his own personal history with her – the fact that three of the nine children in his family died young, and how five of the six who were left entered religious life.

"Like you," he shrewdly writes, "my dear mother tried to see each new departure as a great blessing from God to the family." He assures her that her son is "very happy and contented."

Then, in an effort to allay her fears, Dom James offers graphic descriptions of two extreme and opposing visions of Gethsemani – as a harsh prison (the world's view) and as a bucolic paradise (Dom James' view). Though neither vision is an accurate picture of the place, they provide an intriguing glimpse of the stereotypes of

monastic life at the time: dark and forbidding, on one hand, romanticized and simplistic on the other.

Dom James suggests Mrs. Kelly is confusing Gethsemani as it truly is with Gethsemani as she might be "imagining" it: "A big prison, iron bars on all the windows, monks going around as thin as ghosts, and the abbot with a big long beard and an iron face and a granite heart."

Mona Kelly, Fr. Timothy's mother, with Dom James Fox.

"But wait till you come and visit us, dear Mrs. Kelly!" he reassures her. "You are going to get the surprise of your life when you see the beautiful country and surrounding scenery, wide open stretches of forest, field and farm. And when you see all the young monks going around with beautiful smiles, and then the abbot! He isn't such a bad fellow either."

203

Whether she bought his argument or simply gave up the fight, Fr. Timothy stayed put at Gethsemani. He made his simple vows as a Trappist in 1960, the year his father died, and his solemn vows in 1964. He was ordained a priest on June 12, 1965.

Fr. Timothy can remember overhearing his parents discuss his Trappist vocation – and his stubbornness – shortly before he left Canada for Gethsemani in 1958.

"I was home for a couple of weeks, trying to win their favor. We lived in a big, old, white frame house, so I painted it for them. I happened to be painting just outside the window one day, when my mother and father were in the kitchen. They didn't know I was there. My mother said: ' Well he's *just* going to be a novice. He can come back.' And my father said: 'He's too damned bull-headed to ever come back.' And my mother said: 'Well, you know where he gets that, don't you?'"

Fr. Timothy laughed very hard as he recalled that incident during a conversation in his office not long before the celebration of his 25th anniversary as abbot. As light streamed into the room from a window at his side, he lifted his shoulders ever so slightly, as if to accommodate the weight of time, and added: "They were never resigned to my coming here."

THERE IS A STORY FR. TIMOTHY OFTEN TELLS WHEN he's asked to share his memories of Gethsemani's most illustrious monk, Thomas Merton.

"When I arrived here I spent a week in the guest house, working around. One day they told me the novice master would see me in my room at 6:30. He came in and introduced himself as 'the novice master.' He asked the usual questions, and then he said, 'Well,

what do you know about the life?' I said I had read all of Merton and all of Raymond. He said, 'And what did you think of it?' I said, 'Well, they're both romantic in their presentation. I like Merton's style a lot more and find him asking more profound questions.' And he said, 'Yeah, you really have to be careful what you read.'

"The next morning I come downstairs and the guestmaster said, 'Well, did you meet Thomas Merton?' I said, 'No, I met the novice master.' He said, 'Well, that's Thomas Merton.'"

And that is how Fr. Timothy met Thomas Merton. The story speaks not only to the writer's innate playfulness but to the abbot's incorrigible candor.

It was late August when Fr. Timothy arrived, the least comfortable time of year in Kentucky. The abbey was hot, humid and very crowded, as he recalls:

"The community would've been some 200-plus men at that time. It was a busy place. Just a lot of things going on. It was a full life in the sense of time-consuming work, every minute accounted for. As a novice, I spent a lot of time cleaning in the church, a lot of gardening work, and – in the winter time – cutting trees from the forest."

A decade later, when his stint in Rome was finally over, Fr. Timothy returned to a far different community from the one he had come to as a novice in 1958. Dom James was by then a hermit. Fr. Flavian, a former hermit, was abbot. And Merton was just weeks away from leaving Gethsemani for a tour of Asia, the trip that would take him to his death in Bangkok.

Much had changed, and much would continue to change.

"When I left, there was still the Latin liturgy. We

Fr. Timothy at his ordination in 1965.

were still silent. We used sign language," he said. "I came back to a community that was more communicative. The liturgy was completely different because of English. The church had been renovated, and we had a new abbot."

After years of education and training in Rome, he returned to Gethsemani to package cheese and teach moral theology. "I should have come back to the novitiate," he says, laughing. "I think, in retrospect, it took a while to adjust."

But not too long. Fr. Timothy was soon expressing the voice of dissent in discussions of Fr. Flavian's projects just as he had objected to some of Dom James' proposals. In particular, he opposed the Keith Hollow plan and other strategies to promote the hermit life.

Four years later, when Fr. Flavian announced his intention to resign, Fr. Timothy was Gethsemani's novice master. His name was immediately put forward as a possible successor to Fr. Flavian.

"I really didn't want it. I was young. I was 37," he recalls. "It was more typical to elect men in their mid-40s."

But Fr. Flavian had broken that pattern when he was elected at the age of 36. Nothing stood in the way of Fr. Timothy's election. And so, in March of 1973, he became the eighth abbot of Gethsemani.

"Of course, when I took over I knew exactly what should be done – what everyone should do, how they should be doing it," he recalls, mocking his own youthful naiveté. "Now more than 20 years later, I haven't the vaguest idea."

WITH THE ELECTION OF FR. TIMOTHY, BIG CHANGES were once again in store for the Abbey of Gethsemani.

The community's best-known monk was now five years dead, and with him went the stream of celebrity writers and artists who used to wander up to Merton's hermitage on a fairly regular basis. Fr. Flavian's efforts to quiet down Gethsemani had worked. Now the war in Vietnam was almost over, and the reforms of the 1960s were coming to fruition within the Church and the culture at large.

The monastery, which had lost many of its men during the previous five years, was searching once again for peace in the midst of paradox. The community was in need of balance. The choices seemed extreme. On one end of the spectrum, there was the hermit spirituality that Fr. Flavian had cultivated; at the other end, loomed the increasingly computer-driven mail-order business set up by Dom James. In the background, fading fast, there was the classic ideal of Cistercian agrarian life.

At a time of uncertainty, Fr. Timothy came on strong.

"Some people found Timothy a bit tough at first," recalls Br. Paul Quenon. "He doesn't play games. He just says what he thinks. He was young and energetic – and he still is."

Fr. Timothy remembers the sea change that took place in his life after his election as abbot.

"Gethsemani expects a lot from its abbots. The day before I was elected, I could tell the farm boss something and he'd laugh in my face. The day after I was elected, I was suddenly an expert on raising cows, selling cheese, the mystical life, caring for aging people in an infirmary." He smiles. "That's not quite so."

Fr. Timothy soon became known as a consensus

seeker: an abbot who knows how to build momentum on projects — when to insist, when to resist and when to desist. Building on what Fr. Flavian had begun, Fr. Timothy gave the community a great deal of control over its own decisions and also encouraged individuals within the community to take responsibility for their personal choices, spiritual and otherwise.

"I would say there is still obedience at Gethsemani, but there's also a sharing in the decision-making process," says Jack Ford, a Louisville educator and friend of Merton who in the past has taught classes in philosophy at the monastery.

differed significantly from his predecessors. One of his monks described the difference this way: "All the abbots had aristocratic styles until Timothy came along. They ruled from the front office. Timothy rules from the street."

In the past, Dom James, for example, might go through periods when he would work alongside his monks at their jobs. But both he and Fr. Flavian were more likely to spend their time in their offices.

Timothy, on the other hand, takes his turn serving tables in the refectory. When the monastery still had a working farm, he ran the tractor, picked up the hay, whatever needed to be done. His preference is not to use the telephone to communicate with his monks on the job. He prefers to seek out the person and talk to him face to face. He attends business meetings. He keeps in touch with his committees. He has a sign-up system for making himself available for counsel. He's known for being a good listener, a wise judge of his monks' talents and an approachable leader.

"I think this is something that's desperately needed in the church. I think at some point there has to be authority, but it has to be authority designated by community. I think Timothy is very sensitive to this."

When he moved into the abbot's office, Fr. Timothy's priority was the community life of his monks, rather than the construction of buildings or the launching of business plans.

"I think I was most interested in individual brothers, in the sense that they be respected and encouraged and that their human space be recognized," he said. "I trusted their competence in their own vocations and did not feel they had to do it exactly as I would do it."

The way Fr. Timothy dealt with the community

"Timothy is really very good about arranging things in the monastery so that each of the different individuals here can exercise their talents and still be a monk," says Br. Frederic Collins.

"And believe me that's not easy to do. All 70 of us are contemplative monks, but there's a tremendous range from very quiet to very active people."

THE ABBACY OF FATHER TIMOTHY

1973: Fr. Timothy is elected eighth abbot of Gethsemani; infirmary completed.

1975: Fall of Saigon, end of Vietnam War.

1978: Community sells milking herd and switches to beef operation.

1982: The first artificial heart is implanted.

1989: Renovation of retreat house, which opens to women.

1991: Persian Gulf War erupts.

1996: Trappists in Algeria are murdered in rebel attack; Dalai Lama visits during international Gethsemani Encounter.

1997: Mother Teresa dies.

1998: 900th anniversary of Cistercian Order, 150th anniversary of Abbey of Gethsemani, 30th anniversary of Merton's death, and 25th anniversary of Fr. Timothy's installation as abbot.

BROTHER PATRICK HART, THE ABBOT'S SECRETARY, TELLS a story about life at Gethsemani that ought to dispel anybody's romantic notion that time stands still at the oldest Trappist monastery in America.

"I think it was Frederic Dunne who said it helps to create community interest if you build or tear down something every year – even if it's only a chicken coop," Br. Patrick says.

When Fr. Timothy became abbot, the choice of what to build was already made for him. The construction of a new 14-room infirmary building, north of the monastery complex, was well underway. And though he

OPPOSITE: *Joe Ritchie, supervisor of the guesthouse renovation, with a weathervane that sat atop the church steeple for a time.* LEFT: *The guesthouse under renovation.*

had no construction plans in mind, other than completing the infirmary, he knew that down the road the next big project would be a major overhaul of the retreat house.

During Fr. Flavian's tenure as abbot, the longtime Gethsemani tradition of weekend retreats for men had been scaled back dramatically.

"Partially it was just his own perception of monastic life," says Fr. Timothy, " but partially, too, it was because in those days after Vatican II, retreats were more family-oriented. We didn't fit into that picture."

But by the 1980s, private retreats were growing more popular both in the church and in the culture at large. Drawing on the Cistercian principle of hospitality, Fr. Timothy proposed modernizing the facility to make it a more inviting place for spiritual retreat.

"I just thought the times were dictating that monastic life could be shared," he recalls. And by shared, Fr. Timothy truly meant *shared*.

He proposed opening up the retreat house to women – a resounding break with Gethsemani tradition. Some of his monks were against the idea, arguing that a female presence in the retreat house would pose far more disadvantages to the community than it would offer benefits to women. Fr. Timothy disagreed.

The question came to a head during the renovation process, when the original design called for common washrooms to be shared by retreatants. Fr. Timothy objected, and others who were involved in the project agreed with him that private baths attached to each room were preferable. Once the building was equipped with private baths, there was no other obstacle in the way of opening it up to women.

There were a number of solid reasons for welcoming women to the retreat house, and one of them was their generosity. The retreat house renovation – unlike other construction projects at the abbey – was paid for by donations, and women were among the big givers.

"I said over and over, we have to do something to respect that. If we are going to accept their generosity, we have to give them something in return," Fr. Timothy said. Jack Ford remembers a strong suggestion by Jane Morton Norton, a Louisville philanthropist who contributed to the renovation fund, that women be allowed to stay in the facility they helped to build.

Indeed, in June 1989, shortly after the retreat house

re-opened, women were invited to make retreats one week out of each month. But when it became clear that there was a demand for more time, an alternating schedule was arranged that allowed women two weeks each month. Despite initial misgivings, the plan has worked well, according to Fr. Timothy.

"Part of the reason we alternate is that if it were open to them every week, I think we'd be inundated with women. I don't mean that pejoratively. It's just that women are, shall we say, more spiritually inclined," he said. As it is, the time set aside for women fills up so fast that, for all but a few weeks of the year, reservations must be made at least 12 months in advance.

The renovated retreat house now draws guests from all over the world – some 3,000 a year. There is no set fee for staying there: retreatants are simply asked to leave a donation in whatever size they deem appropriate.

There's usually a mix of young and old in the house at any given time. On the average, one in four retreatants is not Catholic. It is not unusual for Jews, Buddhists, even non-believers to make retreats at Gethsemani.

Brother Luke Armour, who served as guestmaster soon after the retreat house re-opened, believes many people come to Gethsemani simply for a quiet place to be alone. "My guess is that the culture is so over-stimulated that this offers refreshment without rival," he said. "There are no expectations here. No place to go, and all day to get there."

Retreats are self-directed. Though the guestmaster and the abbey chaplain are available for conferences on request, no one monitors a retreatant's activities. An individual may choose to hike among the 1,000 acres of monastic land across the road from the monastery, read in her private room or the retreat house library, pray privately in the church or guest chapel, or chant psalms with the monks in church. The only "rule" retreatants are asked to follow is silence.

"The guests are really quite respectful of our life,"

Fr. Timothy said. During his abbacy, seating for visitors at Mass was moved from the rear of the church, where it had been for more than a century, to the front where the monks sat.

"Certainly when we moved the people to the front of the church for the Eucharist, it was a big step," Fr. Timothy said. "It was done with a lot of suffering for some of the brothers. Yet they've accepted it, and it does enrich the liturgy."

Father Felix Donahue served as retreat chaplain at Gethsemani prior to 1990, when he was elected superior of the Trappist monastery at Novo Mundo in Brazil. He said "the very presence" of retreatants is positive feedback for monks.

"It's really a two-way street. We gain by the example of busy people – parents who make time to spend the weekend or a week in a monastery. They don't have to do it. They've got other things to do. Nobody is making them get up at 3 for Vigils or turn out for Mass or keep reasonably quiet. I feel I receive life from these people."

The retreat house was not the only target of renovation and reform in Fr. Timothy's plan. The project also included a redesign of the front of the church, a new guest chapel, installation of a series of stained-glass windows in the south wall of the church and the placement of a new organ in the center of the

choir. Soon after it was completed, the project –
designed by Louisville's Potter and Cox Architects – was
awarded a Kentucky Society of Architects Honor
Award for Design Excellence. It has been Fr. Timothy's
signature building project.

OPPOSITE: *Nuns on St. Joseph's Hill, the former site of Gethsemani College.*
LEFT: *Dom Frederic Dunne in the days before Gethsemani was opened to women retreatants.*

GETHSEMANI'S NEW POLICY ALLOWING WOMEN TO make retreats was generally well accepted by the community.

"It's been for the good," says Fr. Matthew. "It makes relations with women much more normal." Prior to that, of course, women were not seen at the abbey a great deal; although – as the story of the visit of Gov. Beckham's wife illustrated – they were included at special occasions as far back as Dom Edmond's day.

Fr. Matthew recalls that the first woman to enter the monastic enclosure, uninvited, was a driver for United Parcel Service.

"She drove in one day around the back to the Farms Building, and the monks looked at her and said, 'Hey! Hey!' And they called UPS and said, 'Don't do that again!' But since then, they don't worry about it. Nurses come in. Therapists. It's much more normal, I think, and healthier."

213

Gethsemani's openness to women took a dramatic turn in the 1990s when two Trappistine nuns were welcomed into the community temporarily to live as monks. The first was Sister Catharina Shibuya, of Nasu in Japan, who stayed for 10 months while brushing up on her English in preparation for a job as a translator for the General Chapter.

More recently, Sister Maricela Garcia lived at Gethsemani for three years. A Mexican-born nun of Our Lady of the Redwoods Monastery in northern California, she came to Kentucky for an extended monastic retreat.

In both cases, Gethsemani showed remarkable generosity and flexibility. A community of men who less than a decade earlier had worried about the presence of female retreatants now welcomed female monks to live among them as temporary members of their community.

An accomplished seamstress, Sr. Maricela served as a tailor for the monks during her stay. A small woman with dark eyes and a generous smile, her appearance in choir, wearing the same habit as her brothers, or on duty at the desk of the retreat house lobby sometimes startled visitors to the abbey.

The monks, however, took her presence in stride.

"I owe a debt of gratitude to the whole community," Sr. Maricela said. "I think it is pretty mature in some ways to receive me and to allow me to stay here for so long. It has worked well because they know how to treat me. I find the experience very enriching for me, and I believe it is also for them."

At a time when the Church at large grapples with issues of justice and equality within its own ranks, Gethsemani's welcoming of Sr. Maricela stands as a reminder that even the most intimidating obstacles can be overcome when they are handled in a spirit of brotherly — and sisterly — love.

Sr. Maricela spoke with candor and affection about her experiences at Gethsemani: "I really never felt odd because I knew what I was here for. We come to the monastery not to hide ourselves but to become the humans that we truly are."

She said she learned a great deal about "tolerance" from the monks of Gethsemani: "The beauty is they respect each other even when they have totally different theological backgrounds. I really never have heard them raise their voices against each other."

To most observers, her story would stand out as an extraordinary chapter in the 150-year-old history of the abbey, but Sr. Maricela insists it has been as simple and ordinary as any experience in the life of a Trappist.

"I don't see the monks as just a community of men, but as a community of monastic people with the same issues as women and the same aim — to lead the monastic life," she said.

For a century, Gethsemani had sustained itself by farming. By the late 1970s, however, the community's primary financial support came from its thriving mail-order food business. Agriculture was becoming a less feasible source of income for the community, which had dwindled in size and no longer could supply the manpower needed to keep a working farm afloat.

"I was always very dedicated to the farm, but also a realist," Fr. Timothy said. "Looking at the financial reports it was clear we'd have to get away from that."

Years earlier, the monastery had sold its herd of

Duroc hogs, which had supplied such popular Gethsemani Farms products as sausage, ham and bacon. Then in 1978, Fr. Timothy sold the abbey's blue-ribbon herd of milking cows and began buying all the milk necessary for the production of cheese. For a time, the monks had beef cattle but eventually that herd was also sold. The acreage that was still being worked by monks was leased to local farmers. Currently there are about 350 acres of row crops and 100 acres of hay being cultivated on monastery land. Approximately 1,400 acres of woodland, once cut by monks for lumber, are now being rebuilt under a reforesting plan. And the monks themselves still maintain a large vegetable garden behind the enclosure walls.

The monastery's mail-order business has grown considerably during the 25 years Fr. Timothy has been in office. A carefully cultivated customer list bears more than 100,000 names today, and a monastery-wide computer network has established Gethsemani Farms as a well-equipped competitor in the post-modern world of instant communication.

With remarkably little noise or commotion, the production of food products is carried out six days a week — even on national holidays but never on Catholic feast days. In the bakery, monks bake hundreds of fruitcakes daily from the first of January until the first of December. By hand, they place California walnuts and Georgia pecans in the tops of the fruitcakes as they cool. In

Gethsemani Farms:
How a Monastery Supports Itself

All Gethsemani Farms products are available by mail order. The Trappists produce three varieties of Port du Salut cheese in sizes ranging from wedge to wheel, fruitcakes baked by hand and Kentucky bourbon fudge. Opposite: A chart compares the abbey's overall budget in 1952, the first full year of operation of Gethsemani Farms, to that of 1997.

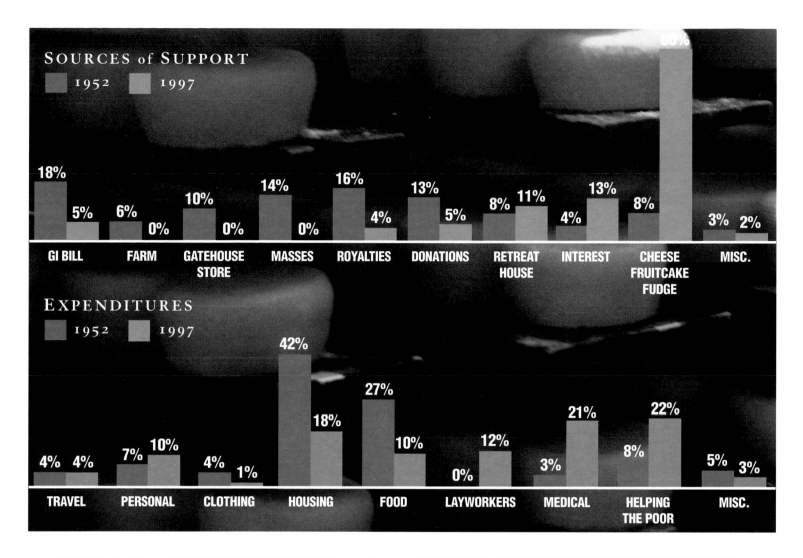

SOURCES of SUPPORT
■ 1952 ■ 1997

GI BILL	FARM	GATEHOUSE STORE	MASSES	ROYALTIES	DONATIONS	RETREAT HOUSE	INTEREST	CHEESE FRUITCAKE FUDGE	MISC.
18%	6%	10%	14%	16%	13%	8%	13%	8%	3%
5%	0%	0%	0%	4%	5%	11%	4%	60%	2%

EXPENDITURES
■ 1952 ■ 1997

TRAVEL	PERSONAL	CLOTHING	HOUSING	FOOD	LAYWORKERS	MEDICAL	HELPING THE POOR	MISC.
4%	7%	4%	42%	27%	0%	3%	8%	5%
4%	10%	1%	18%	10%	12%	21%	22%	3%

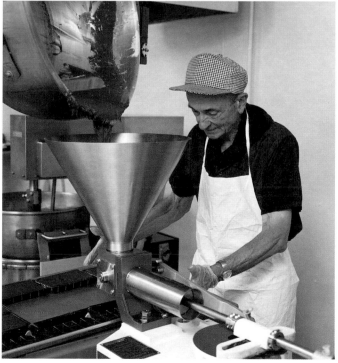

another room, monks produce Kentucky bourbon fudge, based on a recipe created by a dentist from nearby Bardstown. Although fruitcake was the monastery's best-selling item for years, its popularity has been eclipsed by the fudge.

Monks also produce three varieties of Port du Salut cheese – mild, aged and smoked – in sizes ranging from wedge to wheel. All products are available by mail order, with a peak season that begins in November and continues, at a breakneck pace, right up to the last week in Advent.

Gethsemani Farms experienced a record high in sales in 1997, a cause for thanksgiving at the monastery. A thriving business means a financially secure monastery, or as Br. Luke said, "It puts chow on the table."

But record sales also mean a greater pool of funds for the many civic and religious charities sponsored by Gethsemani. To distribute those funds, the monastery today employs two female administrators with longtime experience working with low-income residents of the region.

Br. Frederic was in charge of Gethsemani's charitable projects for many years. He helped get Habitat for Humanity established in the three-county area surrounding Gethsemani and has served on its board and as its treasurer. He said he became involved with that aspect of the monastery's finances in the 1960s, in part "to ease my conscience about living in a relatively affluent monastery and being treasurer and doing all the things the treasurer has to do to keep this place solid."

Br. Frederic was among the first group of monks from Gethsemani to go to the Monastery of Miraflores in Chile in 1966. He volunteered, looking forward to a life of poverty and austerity.

"I went down there for three years, and lo and behold I found out that the monastery there had a bigger piece of property than we had here. Proportionately they had really nice buildings. We lived near poor people and had poor people working for us, but we were really affluent Americans in a poor country. Besides, I was already in my 40s. I wasn't learning Spanish that well. I decided to come back to Gethsemani."

Br. Frederic still longed to live a simple life in a small community, however. Fr. Flavian, who was abbot at the time, was sympathetic, but he asked Br. Frederic to serve in the treasurer's office, temporarily, while he sorted out what he wanted to do next. Although Br. Frederic visited several small monasteries around the country, he ended up staying at Gethsemani in the treasurer's office.

"I think it was providential I did stay," he said. "Since we have been successful in earning money,

enough to support ourselves – and that's one of the principles of this monastery, to be self-supporting – we make enough extra and receive donations and money from various places that it allows us to have a very generous budget for helping the poor. Fr. Timothy is pleased with that."

GENEROUS BENEFACTORS HAVE EMERGED IN NEARLY every generation of Gethsemani's life, providing support for the community's growing needs.

After World War II, a diverse group of patrons was instrumental in funding some of the abbey's most significant ventures. Captain James Kinnarney of Louisville, for example, helped get the monastery's first two foundations on their feet in the late 1940s. Through the generosity of Mrs. Mazie Froedtert of Milwaukee, the monastery was able to expand its acreage and improve the buildings on it. Among other things, Mrs. Froedtert funded the construction of a large silo and the present sacristy, the installation of an infirmary elevator and the addition of a large farm to the monastery's holdings. Jim Stanton of Washington, D.C., brother of Gethsemani's Brother Nivard, and Mrs. Jane Morton Norton of Louisville were both major supporters of the retreat house renovation.

The Skakel family of Connecticut, who befriended Gethsemani while Dom James was abbot, has remained a generous benefactor into Fr. Timothy's tenure. George Skakel is credited with first suggesting to Dom James that the monastery shift its emphasis from farming to cheese-making.

"He took a look at our farm and said we could never sustain 250 monks on this pile of rocks," Br. Patrick said. "He said we needed some kind of industry and suggested cheese."

The Skakel chapel, built at the time of the retreat house renovation, is one of many examples of the family's continued interest in the abbey.

THE CISTERCIAN JUBILEE YEAR OF 1998 WAS LONG anticipated at the Abbey of Gethsemani. It would be a year of noteworthy anniversaries for the community: 900 years since the founding of the Cistercian Order at Citeaux; 150 years of Trappists in Kentucky; 30 years since Merton's death in Bangkok, and 25 years of Fr. Timothy's abbacy.

A series of carefully planned liturgies and public celebrations began in earnest in February with a banquet (and roast) in honor of Fr. Timothy's anniversary during the regional meeting of North American Trappist abbots and abbesses.

By year's end, Gethsemani would also host a commemoration of the 1872 dedication of the monastery in March; a celebration of Gethsemani's presence in Kentucky with the religious of the area in June; an open house for neighbors in July; a luncheon for former brothers and their families in August; a monastic conference in October; a special service and procession in memory of Gethsemani's deceased founders and forebears on All Souls' Day; a celebration of the anniversary of the dedication of the Church on November 15; a guest lecture on the anniversary of Merton's death in December; and a closing ceremony in honor of the founders of Gethsemani on December 21, attended by the Abbot General, the Abbot of Melleray, the abbots of the daughterhouses and the clergy of the Archdiocese of Louisville.

Clearly it would be a year of reflection on the past and anticipation of the future. In the midst of the planning, Fr. Timothy spoke eloquently of the goals that he hoped to accomplish in the remaining years of his abbacy.

"One goal is to continue to respect individual persons in the community and their individual vocations," he said. "The eastern tradition has a word for it – *idiorhythmic* – which means each one establishes his own rhythm yet still lives it out in the community context.

IN 1909, DOM EDMOND REPLACED THE PLAIN WINDOWS IN GETHSEMANI'S CHURCH WITH 23 STAINED-GLASS PANELS CUSTOM-DESIGNED BY THE MEYER FIRM OF MUNICH, GERMANY. IN 1923, HE ADDED 11 WINDOWS FROM MUNICH'S ZETTLER FIRM.

WHEN THE CHURCH WAS RENOVATED 40 YEARS LATER, THE REDESIGN EMPHASIZED SIMPLICITY AND LIGHT. THE DARKLY EXPRESSIVE MUNICH WINDOWS WERE GIVEN AWAY AND REPLACED WITH PALE GLASS IN ABSTRACT PATTERNS. IN 1997, THE ABBEY LEARNED A KENTUCKY FAMILY POSSESSED THE OLD WINDOWS AND WISHED TO RETURN THEM. BUT BY THEN, THE YEARS HAD TAKEN THEIR TOLL, AND MOST OF THE WINDOWS WERE IN PIECES.

WITH THE HELP OF VOLUNTEERS AND PROFESSIONALS, THE MONKS BEGAN PAINSTAKINGLY PUTTING THE PIECES BACK TOGETHER. AMONG THE REASSEMBLED WINDOWS WAS THE "THE SALVE WINDOW," REPRESENTING OUR LADY, MOTHER OF CISTERCIANS, WHICH ORIGINALLY WAS LOCATED BEHIND THE MAIN ALTAR.

This has to be done with a lot of real, honest spiritual discernment."

Fr. Timothy said he also hopes the community can find a replacement for the psychological and physical void created by the phasing out of farming at Gethsemani.

"To be celibate, honestly, there has to be this element of caring for something. A married couple cares for one

220

another. In our context, caring for the land, caring for a farm, provided a lot of that. We really have to find a replacement for it," he said.

He said the community also needs to find better ways to share its prayer life with the broader community, either through example or encouragement. "There are so many people looking for the same thing we are looking for," Fr. Timothy said, "and there are ways we can support one another, encourage one another."

He said he believes the greatest challenge facing Gethsemani and Cistercians in general is essentially the same one facing the church at large – that is, the challenge of multiculturalism.

"When we introduce monastic life to other cultures, like in Africa, we have to understand that a way of life that we find very simple is actually very complex in another culture. It was originally thought the life is lived the same way in every house. But to ask people in the Philippines or in Africa to live precisely the way we do here at Gethsemani is rather difficult nowadays. Making those adaptations is a challenge," he said.

"As Westerners we have such a temptation to think our way is best. But communities in the Far East – Japan, Hong Kong, Philippines, and so on – have lots of life in them. The Japanese, for example, are beginning to realize they have their own traditions that are far more adaptable to their culture than just adopting the Western model and being faithful to it."

Fr. Timothy and the Dalai Lama, exiled leader of Tibet, during an historic 1996 meeting of Buddhist and Christian monastics at Gethsemani.

Fr. Timothy has supported his own monks' efforts to bring about greater understanding between Eastern and Western monasticism. To that end, the Dalai Lama, the exiled leader of Tibet and a friend of Merton, has visited Gethsemani twice in the 1990s. Most recently, he participated in the 1996 Gethsemani Encounter, an historic five-day meeting of Buddhist and Christian monastics. The Dalai Lama had suggested that the meeting be held in a monastery, where he could be "a monk among monks," and the choice of Gethsemani, his old friend's home, pleased him greatly. Some 50 monks and nuns from around the world attended the conference to discuss the similarities and differences in their spiritual traditions.

When dealing with multicultural issues, the international character of the Cistercian Order offers built-in advantages. To illustrate that point, Fr. Timothy tells the story of how the French monks of the Abbey of Melleray, Gethsemani's motherhouse, rejected the American monks in the aftermath of the 19th-century college scandal, dismissing them as "rebellious monks" out of touch with Cistercian principles.

"They wanted nothing to do with them," Fr. Timothy said. "Another house, Oelenberg in Alsace, took us over temporarily, and that's when Edmond Obrecht came. He was first appointed superior by the General Chapter, then elected.

"That's still in my memory because at one of my first General Chapters, I raised the question of the value of an international order, and a fellow abbot said, 'My young father does not have a very good understanding of history.' He said, 'If it were not for ours being an international order, Gethsemani would not even exist today.' "

Fr. Timothy said he would like to see Gethsemani develop a more serious intellectual life in years to come. "Not that I am an intellectual by nature," he said, "but just reading monastic history, I can see that during those periods when communities were intellectually aware, they were better off all around.

"We've continued to have outside speakers and so on, but as a community, as individuals, we could do better. I just haven't found a way to encourage that," he said.

He said a deeper intellectual life would include an investigation of new models for monastic life and an exploration of how better to live out the values reflected in the Gospel.

Fr. Timothy is keenly aware of the reputation that proceeds an abbot of Gethsemani, and likes to illustrate the weight of that reputation by recounting an incident that took place in a Louisville hospital not long after he had been elected abbot. He was there to visit one of his monks.

"An old sister there said to me, 'Are you from Gethsemani?' She said she knew Abbot Obrecht, and she remembered he was such a great man. She remembered Abbot Dunne, such a holy man, and Abbot Fox, such a great man. And Abbot Burns was now become a hermit, and such a holy man. And then she said, 'Who's abbot now?' And I said, 'Well I am.' And she said, 'YOU? But they were such distinguished men.' "

As abbot of Gethsemani, Fr. Timothy visits six houses every couple of years, evaluating the tenure of the abbots of his daughterhouses. On three occasions, he decided it was time for an abbot to resign, perhaps against his wishes.

"You ask if there has been any trauma in being abbot? That was it. In all three cases, I would make the same decision . . . but it was definitely traumatic. The third one was the worst one. I was getting a reputation – Watch your scalp – here he comes."

But those experiences also made him aware of the importance of recognizing when his own time comes.

"I really want to know. I want someone to tell me. I assure you I will not put up any fight. That is the strength of the system. It is important to use it as such. It is the most brotherly thing to do."

As the Abbey of Gethsemani heads into a new millennium, Fr. Timothy sees the community at a crossroads. Change will inevitably come about – some of it planned, some of it unexpected and unwanted. How the oldest Trappist monastery in America responds will have a lot to do with the intrinsic spirit of the place, the "charism" or personality that sets it apart from other communities.

Fr. Timothy believes that Gethsemani does have a distinct personality, based in part on an accident of history – its founding on the American frontier by French monks of an ascetic spiritual bent.

"We have a sense of stability based on the size of our cemetery. Stability is a part of our experience as a community. We have a tradition of an austere life and an element of seriousness. I do think there is a warmth and maturity. We accept people into our midst without questioning them a lot about their past."

Because it has long been a large community, there has been a degree of "anonymity and a level of trust" at

Gethsemani that may not exist at smaller monasteries, where privacy is harder to maintain, Fr. Timothy said.

Br. Patrick describes it this way: "You're kind of on top of one another in a smaller community. Here you have space to breathe, to do your own thing – not that everyone's doing that. There's a community spirit. But I think people respect one another. They allow you to be a little off-beat, a little eccentric."

Like it or not, however, since the 1960s, Gethsemani has grown smaller by the decade. The community's younger monks were born after Vatican II. Their memories do not include silence or overcrowding. They are a new breed. They sometimes tire of comparisons to customs and traditions they have never experienced.

Is Gethsemani in for even greater changes than in the past? Will the trust and tolerance that characterize the monastery today be replaced by other qualities in the future?

The abbot who has ruled from the street for a quar-

ter century isn't making any predictions. He prefers to rephrase such a question, to turn it around so that it speaks to issues more at the heart of monastic life.

"We get caught up in preserving the institution and earning our living, and we're here for much, much more – to live a deeper reality. I think that's a little bit of what Merton is perhaps facetiously saying [in his complaints about monastic life]: The problem is, you can get wrapped up in all these other questions rather than wrapped up in the primal reason we're all here."

IN THE END, THE STORY OF THE ABBEY OF GETHSE-mani may be as simple and as confounding as this:

For 150 years, a community of men have made their life in a green valley surrounded by the wooded hills and gently rolling fields of central Kentucky. Every day of those 150 years, in war and blizzard and deepest grief, they have risen in the middle of the night to praise God in the dark together. Tomorrow, they will rise again.

EPILOGUE:
"WHY HAST THOU
COME HERE?"

O N MY FIRST TRIP TO THE ABBEY OF GETHSEMANI, Br. Raphael Prendergast and I drove through the woods in an old white truck to the hermitage where Thomas Merton spent the last years of his life. It is a small cabin built of cinder blocks, now used by monks in need of a quiet week alone to pray and meditate. I recognized it instantly from old photographs: the flat roof and casement windows, the open porch, the logs piled high against the side of the house, the hand-built cross in the yard.

Sitting in the truck, we talked about the place and the man who once lived there. We were careful not to drive too close to the cabin to avoid disturbing the monk on retreat inside. But he heard the truck rumble up the dirt road anyway and motioned to us from the porch to get out and join him.

The sweet scent of incense greeted us at the door. A visiting priest had stopped by to say Mass that morning in the cabin's chapel. I asked the monk who was staying there if it had been quiet during the night, and he told us of hearing coyotes howl and deer rustling past trees close to the house. As we talked, we walked from the front room with its crowded bookshelves, past the kitchen and into a small bedroom with a window opening out to the graceful woods.

The hermitage where Thomas Merton lived the last years of his life.

And then we were back in the truck, Br. Raphael at the wheel, heading for the next stop on our tour of the monastery. There was no way for me to know then that five years later, at work on this book, I would begin my research alone for a few days in that same, small, history-laden cabin. It was a good place from which to start: a poet's refuge, a hermit's hideout, a contemplative's retreat.

As much as any single Trappist of Gethsemani, Merton has shaped the spirit and personality of the monastery he called home. Br. Patrick Hart, Merton's secretary at the time of his death, believes that the abbey's well-known openness to other faith traditions is related in large part to Merton's broad-minded attitudes.

"There is a lack of narrowness and a kind of world vision at work in Merton. He could communicate with Muslims, and he had people like Rabbi Abraham Heschel coming down to visit. And they could just understand one another. Merton said of the Dalai Lama, 'We are spiritual comrades. We understand each other perfectly,' " Br. Patrick said.

He continues, "When it comes to religious differences, we don't concentrate on the little things that divide but on what unites. They say if you go deep enough into your own tradition, there's a kind of bond with others. That's where all of these traditions unite. But you have to go deep."

Going deep is the point of life at Gethsemani. Whether a monk is alone in a hermitage or side by side with his brother scraping carrots in the kitchen or sliding cheese wheels into boxes, the point is to get beneath the surface to the place where God waits in love.

Monks are no better at this process, no better at praying and loving, than any other man or woman. But monastic life gives them the structure and support and encouragement to keep at it even when they fail. And they do.

I remember one monk telling me on that first visit that the monastic life requires nothing more of a person than simply "to be." Then with a smile (or was it a wince?) he added: "That sounds great, until you have to do it."

The monks of Gethsemani believe that God is teaching them who they are, slowly and carefully and sometimes painfully. The contemplative way of life, as one monk explained it to me, is a process that takes you apart and lets you see inside yourself. It's a challenging life, a life whose goal is change.

The outward symbols and metaphors of life at

I SUFFERED THIS FOR YOU, WHAT HAVE YOU DONE FOR ME?

Gethsemani – the trappings of the Trappists, if you will – reflect the deeper process of spiritual conversion going on in each monk's interior life. Traditionally when a man enters the monastery, his hair is shaven, his name taken away and a new one bestowed. His journey begins in self-surrender.

Life at Gethsemani is an inward journey, a circuitous and rigorous route that takes time to travel. It begins when a man signs on as a postulant. During that six-month trial period, he wears street clothes while living the Trappist way of life. His clothing changes as the level of his commitment does: a white robe as a novice; the black scapular and leather belt after making simple vows; the cowl upon his solemn profession.

Throughout the process, the monk seeks to discover his true self.

Jack Ford, a longtime Gethsemani observer, recalls that years ago the monastery's chapter room had a quotation on the wall that asked: *Why hast thou come here?* Ford found the query amusing: "If *they* don't know why they came here, then who among us does?"

Later it struck him that the question was not frivolous or redundant but absolutely essential. He saw it as the question every individual needs to ask daily: "Because if you don't, well, it's like going down the street every day and the houses are there and after a while you don't see them anymore. It becomes so routine you take it for granted."

It is a monk's job to be aware of why he has come to a monastery and, by example and through prayer, to lead others to that awareness.

In the post-Vatican II Church, monks are encouraged to build bridges between monasticism and the rest of the world. Each has lessons to teach the other. Ford has been making retreats at Geth-

Opposite: *The solemn profession of a monk, when he takes his final vows.*
Above: *The Blessing of the Graves, an All Souls' Day ritual.*

semani for 50 years, and over that period of time his perceptions of monastic life – and his participation in it – have changed dramatically.

"There's far less of a wall between the two worlds," Ford says. "I don't dispute that we have different vocations, but at the same time I see more common movement and interest and sharing than I would have ever suspected. Before, I thought we were doing two radically different things, but now I see we're doing *different* things but not radically different."

How else can it be explained that thousands of retreatants pack the guest rooms at Gethsemani each year? If there were no common ground between the two ways of life, no lessons to be shared, why would there be such a strong and persistent attraction to such an out-of-the-way place?

Perhaps the greatest paradox of life at Gethsemani is that men who have freely chosen not to assert themselves in the world are, on a daily basis, exercising greater influence on that world than if they had remained within it.

Cistercian monks make three vows at the time of their profession: obedience, stability and conversion of manners – the last of those encompassing the traditional vows of poverty and chastity. Merton said the whole meaning of a monk's life is summed up in these promises. Paradoxically, the vows "deliver him from the uncertainties and cares and illusions that beset the man of the world" at the very same time that they "imply struggle and difficulty."

A novice may take up to nine years to make his per-

manent commitment to the Trappist life at Gethsemani. After that, a decision to further delay is a decision to leave. As with any way of life, some come to the monastery to work out problems, others to avoid them. Either way, their problems accompany them. As a way of identifying those who are poor prospects for the life, all candidates are given psychological tests. Age limits are imposed: those under 22 or over 45 are generally considered bad risks for adapting to the rigors and restrictions of the monastic vows.

Gethsemani looks for men with healthy self-esteem, an ability to accept limits on their personal freedom and an understanding of love as something far deeper and more mysterious than mere emotion. Monastic life is often called "a school for charity," and it's true that it

LEFT: *An aerial view of the monks' cemetery at Gethsemani, and the burial of a monk.*
OPPOSITE: *Monks and visitors entering the abbey church by candlelight for the Easter Vigil Mass.*

communicate the hazards of the monk's path. "For it is one thing to see the land of peace from a wooded ridge," he wrote, ". . . and another to tread the road that leads to it."

A proverb of the Desert Fathers also applies here. Abbot Bessarion, as he was dying, said, "A monk should be all eye, like the cherubim and seraphim." There is no place to hide in monastic life – no way not to see or be seen. Some will dismiss it as a form of escape from the world, a place for spiritual runaways, but the life of a monk is actually grounded in radically interdependent human relationships and an all-encompassing trust in God.

requires, above all, insight into the meaning of love. As a vocations director for the community once told me, the true monk understands love as the desire "to share your life with others and to suffer the consequences of that."

In terms of creature comforts, life at Gethsemani today is not as hard as it has been in the past. Private rooms, telephones, the Internet – what would Gethsemani's founders think if they toured their monastery today? Yet it is still a hard life.

St. Augustine, writing in the 5th century, used understatement and a metaphor from nature to

THE ORGANIZATION OF THE CISTERCIAN ORDER IS BASED on the principle of self-rule. Each monastery has a great deal of autonomy. The central authority of the order is the General Chapter, the legislative assembly of abbots that convenes in France every few years. The decisions made by the abbots are then carried out by the Abbot General, the elected chief executive of the order. He is accountable to the abbots for the decisions he makes between General Chapters.

"In actual fact, he could not tell Gethsemani: 'You send X-number of dollars to help somebody, or you send two monks someplace.' He has no authority within the Gethsemani community. He could ask if Gethsemani would be willing to do something. It is a little different set-up from most religious organizations," Fr. Timothy said.

Cistercians today are responsible for more than 250 abbeys worldwide. From their ranks have come two popes, 40 canonized saints, dozens of cardinals and many bishops. It is a complex, multi-cultural, pluralistic, international organization.

Yet, as a tradition lived out in a place like Gethsemani, it is as straightforward as a casket-less burial, as simple as a psalm, as basic as fire struck from rock on the eve of Easter.

IN HER LATEST VOLUME OF *Conversations with Kentucky Writers,* L. Elisabeth Beattie asks the commonwealth's distinguished historian, Thomas D. Clark, whether he has an audience in mind when he writes.

"Never historians!" he shoots back. "That's an abomination in the sight of God. Historians writing for historians. That's digging up a corpse out of one grave and burying it in another. No, I have an interested

TOP: *Bronze statues in the woods.*

reader in my writing. I've always seen some faces across the typewriter, just ordinary people."

In writing this book, I, too, see certain faces across my keyboard in the distance beyond my computer screen.

I see faces of the women and men I sit by at breakfast and stand beside at Compline when I am on retreat at Gethsemani.

I see faces of monks – some ordinary, some extraordinary – who have shared their memories and opened their hearts to me. I see us talking in quiet rooms at the retreat house, on paths leading high into the knobs, and from lawn chairs under the trees along the abbey avenue. I see us in a Virginia hermitage and outside a barn in northern Utah. I hear us, too: shouting over the clamor of a sudden Georgia cloudburst and whispering, hands cupped to our mouths, in the dark of a 12th-century church in the Loire Valley of France.

I see faces I have imagined as I deciphered the delicate script and Old World numerals of the immigrant monks of Melleray.

I see faces of people like myself years ago, drawn to the Abbey of Gethsemani and not yet knowing why – faces of Christians and Jews, Buddhists and Hindus, Muslims and all who find themselves seeking a place where, for 150 years and still counting, love really is all there is.

Acknowledgements

In writing this history of Gethsemani, I have drawn upon the support and expertise of a far-flung community of big-hearted people. To all of them, named and unnamed, I wish to express my gratitude for their guidance, encouragement and, in some cases, sheer patience.

First and foremost, I want to thank the monks of Gethsemani for the great gift of their trust. In choosing me – an outsider to their community and a woman – to research and interpret their story, they made a daring break with tradition. In particular, I am grateful to Abbot Timothy Kelly for graciously granting me unfettered access to the abbey's archives.

I am also indebted to the individual monks who opened their hearts and memories to me, sharing spiritual and historical insights that no amount of document searching could have otherwise revealed. Their recollections are the soul of this book.

I would like to recognize Brother Patrick Hart for his judicious editorial advice; Brother Raphael Prendergast and Brother Frederic Collins for their invaluable assistance in my examination of the abbey's business arm, Gethsemani Farms; Father Chrysogonus Waddell for his translation and analysis of Melleray's proposal to make a foundation in Martinique prior to the founding of Gethsemani; Father Felix Donahue for his perspective as a past archivist of Gethsemani; Father Roman Ginn for blessing me with a glimpse of the hermit life; and to Sister Maricela Garcia, of Redwoods, California, for sharing with me her unique perspective as a female monk of Gethsemani.

My dear friend and intrepid collaborator throughout the process has been Brother Joshua Brands, Gethsemani's indefatigable archivist and third superior. It was Brother Josh who conceived the idea of this book, a comprehensive history of Gethsemani that would document, for the first time, events dating from 1950 to the present.

Brother Josh, who has spent most of the past decade organizing and preserving Gethsemani's archival treasures, knew better than anyone what a wealth of material lay in wait for whoever took on that task. I am honored he proposed the idea to me and thankful that he continued to work by my side, helping me sort through thousands of pages of primary material.

No research into the history of Gethsemani would be complete, of course, without a visit to the motherhouse in France. So, in the spring of 1996, Brother Josh and I made the trip. Traveling with us was Gethsemani's employee supervisor, Joe Ritchie, of nearby Bloomfield, Kentucky. With Joe at the wheel and me navigating, we motored across France, touring Cistercian monasteries. Joe made several significant contributions to the project before and after that trip, but if I were to single out the one I most appreciate, it would be his patience in the face of my tendency to misread French highway signs.

At Melleray, we were greeted in the finest Cistercian tradition by the present and former abbots, Dom Gerard Meneust and Dom Jacques Parriaux. I am forever grateful for the opportunity to walk the same path the founders of Gethsemani walked the morning they left Melleray for America, and to pray in the same 12th-century church they called home. I am appreciative as well to Dom Remi Declercq of the nearby Abbey of Port du Salut for his warm hospitality and to Janet Barbot for serving as translator during our visit.

Closer to home, I wish to thank Abbot Leander Dosch of Utah's Holy Trinity Abbey; Abbot Bernard Johnson and the monks of Georgia's Holy Spirit Abbey; and Father Flavian Burns, of Crozet, Virginia, for the warm receptions they gave me when I visited them.

A special word of thanks goes to Father Clyde Crews, who kindly hand-carried a palm-sized volume of Bishop Flaget's diary from a vault in Louisville to a photography studio in southern Indiana so that we might include it in this book. Clyde's legendary status as the premier historian of Kentucky Catholicism is well-deserved. His devotion to the subject has set high standards for those following in his footsteps. I would like to extend my gratitude as well to The Congregation of the Sisters of St. Francis of the Immaculate Conception in Clinton, Iowa, who permitted me to view documents and reprint photographs from their archives. Thanks, too, to Ron Pen, of Lexington, Kentucky, for sharing a fascinating family docu-

Dom Jacques Parriaux, the former abbot of the Abbey of Melleray, with Gethsemani's archivist, Brother Joshua Brands, walking on the grounds of the French motherhouse in March, 1996.

ment, never before included in a Gethsemani history, that offers a glimpse of the personal side of Dom Benedict Berger.

I wish to thank Paul Plaschke and the staff at Plaschke Design Group for their customary splendid performance. In particular, I want to acknowledge our talented book designer, Julie Breeding, for falling in love with this project, as I did, and for never giving it anything less than her absolute dedication. Thanks to Julie's inventiveness, the book achieves a delicate visual balance between homage to Gethsemani's Old World roots and candor about its place in post-modern America.

I am grateful to Carolyn Yetter not only for her sen-

sitive and graceful editing but for the unflappable enthusiasm she brought to the job. Thanks also to Bob Hower for his photographs that capture the spirit of Gethsemani's past as well as its present, and to Ken Eberhart and the folks at Merrick Printing Company for their uncompromising commitment to excellence.

Writing a book has something in common with the hermit life. For long stretches of time, it leads down a solitary path. I wish to thank my family and friends for their patience and understanding during the long silences and separations, and for their unconditional love when I needed it most. In particular, my thanks go to Kate Adamek for her careful reading of my first draft; Mary Lou Hess for the gifts of her art and her heart; and to my colleagues at *The Courier-Journal,* Greg Johnson and Arlene Jacobson, for their support over the years. Thanks to *The Courier-Journal* also for permission to reproduce material from its pages.

In the end, I am most grateful to my husband, Ken Shapero, and our son, Josh, for their faith in me and in this book. You two are my guardian angels; you show me the way. In particular, I am thankful to Ken, my partner in the publication of this book, for leading me always in the right direction. It was he, years ago, who was the first to place a book by Thomas Merton in my hands. As I recall, he said, "You ought to read this." So I did. The rest is this history.

Works Consulted and Suggested

The Annals of Gethsemani. Abbey of Gethsemani Archives.

Allen, William B. *A History of the People Called Monks.* Abbey of Gethsemani Archives.

Amadeus, Father Maria. *The Right Reverend Dom M. Edmond Obrecht, O.C.S.O.* Kentucky: Abbey of Gethsemani, 1937.

Crews, Clyde F. *An American Holy Land.* Louisville: ikonographics, inc., 1987.

Flanagan, Father Raymond. *Burnt Out Incense.* New York: P. J. Kennedy and Sons, 1949.

Flanagan, Father Raymond. *The Less Traveled Road, A Memoir of Dom Mary Frederic Dunne, O.C.S.O., First American Trappist Abbot.* Milwaukee: The Bruce Publishing Company, 1953.

Gethsemani Abbey: Its Foundation and Present State, Trappist, Kentucky: Abbey of Gethsemani, 1899.

Gethsemani Magnificat. Trappist, Kentucky: Abbey of Gethsemani, 1949.

Knecht, Father M. Edward, editor. *Gethsemani Speaks.* Abbey of Gethsemani Archives.

Hart, Brother Patrick, general editor. *The Journals of Thomas Merton.* San Francisco: HarperCollins, 1996-1998.

Hart, Brother Patrick, editor. *Thomas Merton Monk.* London: Hodder and Stoughton, 1974.

Kelty, Father Matthew. *Aspects of the Monastic Calling.* Trappist, Kentucky: Abbey of Gethsemani, 1975.

Kelty, Father Matthew. *Sermons in a Monastery.* Kalamazoo: Cistercian Publications, 1983.

Merton, Thomas. *The Monastic Journey.* Brother Patrick Hart, editor. Kalamazoo: Cistercian Publications, 1992.

Merton, Thomas. *The Seven Storey Mountain.* New York: Harcourt Brace Jovanovich Inc., 1948.

Merton, Thomas. *The Sign of Jonas.* New York: Harcourt Brace Jovanovich Inc., 1953.

Merton, Thomas. *The Waters of Siloe.* New York: Harcourt, Brace and Company, 1949.

Merton, Thomas. *The Wisdom of the Desert: Sayings from the Desert Fathers of the Fourth Century.* New York: New Directions, 1960.

Minogue, Anna C. *Loretto: Annals of the Century.* New York: The American Press, 1912.

Mitchell, Donald W. and James Wiseman, editors. *Gethsemani Encounter.* New York: Continuum, 1997.

Mott, Michael. *The Seven Mountains of Thomas Merton.* Boston: Houghton Mifflin Company, 1984.

Schauinger, J. Herman. *Cathedrals in the Wilderness: The Story of Benedict Joseph Flaget.* Milwaukee: The Bruce Publishing Company, 1952.

The Rule of St. Benedict (RB 1980). Timothy Fry, editor. Collegeville, Minnesota: Liturgical Press, 1981.

Ward, Benedicta, translator. *The Sayings of the Desert Fathers.* Kalamazoo: Cistercian Publications, 1975.

Webb, Benedict. *The Centenary of Catholicity in Kentucky.* Louisville, Kentucky: Chas. Rogers, 1884.

PHOTOGRAPH and ILLUSTRATION CREDITS

ARCHIVIST'S COMMENT: *Unless otherwise noted, all photographs, narratives and other historical material reproduced in this book are either the property of the Abbey of Gethsemani Archives or The Merton Legacy Trust, or the Abbey has received permission to use them.*

The Abbey also wishes to express gratitude to all who, over the past 150 years, have so generously given of their time and work, making the archives the rich source of monastic literature and art that it is today.

– J.B., O.C.S.O.

Artifacts and documents from the Abbey's archives were photographed by Bob Hower.

Index

ABOUT the CONTRIBUTORS

DIANNE APRILE is a writer for *The Louisville Courier-Journal.* Her first book was The *Things We Don't Forget,* a collection of essays. She was the winner of The National Society of Newspaper Columnists' top award in 1994, and her newspaper and magazine reporting has been honored by the Society of Professional Journalists, American Bar Association, American Psychiatric Association and National Women's History Project. She is the recipient of a Kentucky Arts Council fellowship and a writer's grant from the Kentucky Foundation for Women. She lives in Louisville with her husband and son.

BROTHER JOSHUA BRANDS was trained in archival work at St. Mary's College in Kentucky. As archivist of the Abbey of Gethsemani, he helped launch the Gethsemani Archives Project, which resulted in the translation and transcription of the monastery's early French documents. Under his leadership, a major reorganization of the abbey's archives was completed. He has been a monk at Gethsemani since 1989 and is currently third superior of the community.

JULIE BREEDING studied painting at the Boston Museum School. Her book designs include *The Jack Daniels Barbeque Cookbook* and *Churchill Downs: A Documentary History of America's Most Legendary Racetrack.* She is the recipient of design awards from the Advertising Club of Louisville, Art Directors Club of Philadelphia, New York Type Directors Club and International Association of Business Communicators, and won the Printing Industries of America's international award in 1996. She lives in Louisville, where she is senior designer for Plaschke Design Group.